R00007 30875

CHICAGO PUBLIC LIBRARY
HAROLD WASHINGTON LIBRARY CENTER

R0000730875

D1270933

# LULLABIES

LULLABIES

PRINTED BY ROBERT MACLEHOSE & CO. LTD.
AT GLASGOW
IN 12 POINT BASKERVILLE


700 COPIES, OF WHICH 660 ARE FOR SALE
10 COPIES, SPECIALLY BOUND, ARE
SIGNED BY THE EDITOR

# A
# BOOK OF LULLABIES

## 1300-1900

CHOSEN AND EDITED BY

## F. E. BUDD

FOLCROFT LIBRARY EDITIONS / 1975

Ref
PR
1195
.L8
B8
1975
Cop. 1

# A
# BOOK OF LULLABIES

1300-1900

CHOSEN AND EDITED BY
## F. E. BUDD

ERIC PARTRIDGE
AT THE SCHOLARTIS PRESS
THIRTY MUSEUM STREET, LONDON
1930

# PREFATORY NOTE

In the present anthology I have made an attempt to bring together from the last six centuries of English literature a representative collection of the best of our lullabies and cradle-songs. The earlier temporal limit is determined by the occurrence of the oldest extant example in a manuscript written shortly after 1300 ; the later limit has been fixed at 1900 chiefly through considerations of copyright. The arrangement of the poems is strictly chronological. At the conclusion of each poem I have endeavoured to indicate the manuscript or publication in which it first appeared. Apart from certain minor modifications described at the beginning of the Notes, the original spelling has been preserved in poems earlier than 1500, but in later ones, except those in which dialect is deliberately employed, it has been modernised. The punctuation has been modernised throughout. In the early poems the presence of an articulated final *e* or *es* is indicated by two dots over the vowel (*ë*) ; if a participial termination *ed* is to be given full syllabic value in words where to-day it is slurred over, the fact is indicated by a stroke over the *e* (*èd*). Where an author has left his poem without a title, I have supplied one. In these circumstances I did not consider that an Index of Titles would serve any useful purpose.

My gratitude is due to Messrs. William Heinemann, Ltd., for permission to include Swinburne's *Cradle Songs* and to Mr. W. B. Yeats and Messrs. Ernest Benn, Ltd., for permission to include the *Cradle Song* from Mr. Yeats' *Poems*. I regret that I have not been able to trace the holder of the copyright in Symonds' *Christmas Lullaby*, but I trust that my apologies for including the poem without permission will be accepted.

F. E. BUDD.

*May*, 1930.

# CONTENTS

| | PAGE |
|---|---|
| PREFATORY NOTE - - - - - - - - | V |
| INTRODUCTION - - - - - - - - | 1 |
| TEXT - - - - - - - - - - | 26 |
| NOTES - - - - - - - - - - | 120 |
| INDEX OF AUTHORS - - - - - - | 125 |
| INDEX OF FIRST LINES - - - - - - | 126 |

# INTRODUCTION

'Thou must be patient ; we came crying hither.
Thou know'st, the first time that we smell the air,
We wawl, and cry . . .
When we are born, we cry that we are come
To this great stage of fools.'

*King Lear*, iv, vi.

IF, as may reasonably be assumed, English literature of the last twelve centuries be a reliable index
to the development of the national character, then
it appears that the feature of the Anglo-Saxon
temperament which has undergone least modifica-
tion by Christian and foreign cultural influences,
long and steadily exerted, is the taste for melancholy brooding of the type that finds expression in
elegy. Other features, directly inspired by the con-
ditions of life peculiar to the Teutonic heroic age,
have changed or disappeared with the evolution of
fresh spiritual, political or social environments ;
but this, the offspring of a deep-rooted pessimistic
philosophy, endures. Certain aspects of our literature in all its stages since the eighth century reflect
this taste with varying intensity. In the lullabies
of the present anthology it is mirrored as clearly
and continuously as in any series of poems in the
language. The key to which their music is attuned
is that of subdued elegiac lament rather than of
lyric rapture. The spirit that they foster is one of
stoical resignation in the face of impending calamity,
a quality of mind that enables a man to go through
with things even if he sees no prospect of a successful
issue. It is the spirit of Anglo-Saxon heroic and

elegiac poetry, of Shakespearian tragedy, of Hardy's novels. It speaks in the cry of the mad Lear to the blinded Gloucester. And in its essence it is pagan and fatalistic.

To gather from these remarks that a monotonous note of unrelieved melancholy characterises all the lullabies of this collection would, nevertheless, be misleading. On the contrary, several from Elizabethan times onwards are wholly delightful. But the point to be made at the very outset, even at the risk of exaggeration, is that English lullabies are predominantly *serious* poems. They are not nursery rhymes or mere verbal incantations to conjure up sleep. Written by adults for the reading of adults, and in substance often quite beyond the scope of childish comprehension, they are for the most part lyric songs which, under the guise of what has grown to be an established poetic convention, illustrate definite emotional or philosophic attitudes to life based on experiences which fall to the lot of the majority of human beings. In consequence, they have a direct and instant appeal. It might be said of them, as Johnson said of Gray's *Elegy*, that they ' abound with images which find a mirror in every mind, and with sentiments to which every bosom returns an echo.'

For Lear, the wailing of the new-born babe is an expression of its instinctive knowledge of the fate awaiting it in after life. So is it also for the author of our earliest extant lullaby, the fourteenth-century Anglo-Irish *Lollai, lollai, litil child* (1). In this the elegiac note, which becomes particularly poignant when uttered in relation to young children, is fully voiced. The singer is a mother who sadly anticipates the evils that lie in store for her babe already weeping in his cradle. Born in wickedness, and with the consequences of Adam's sin

2

for his only birthright, he is predestined from of
yore—

> ' Ever to lib in sorow,
>     And sich and mourne evere,'

as his elders had done before him while they were
alive. That he should thrive and prosper is re-
garded as too remote a possibility to be considered
seriously. No. With sorrow he came into this
world, with sorrow he shall leave it. Treacherous
and unstable, the world is his 'full foe'; but
through it he is doomed to wander on the pil-
grimage of life until—

> ' Deth ssal com with a blast
>     Ute of a wel dim horre '

to relieve him from further care. Death, at least,
is a certainty :

> ' Whoder thou salt wend,
>     North other est,
> Deth the sal betide
>     With bitter bale in brest.
>         Lollai, lollai, litil child,
>             This wo Adam the wroght,
>         Whan he of the appil ete,
>             And Eve hit him betacht.'

This song is unique among the lullabies of the
fourteenth and fifteenth centuries in so far as it
expresses the feelings of a purely human mother
towards her babe. The others of the period, and
they are more numerous and in many respects more
beautiful than those of any succeeding age, are
religious lullabies concerned for the most part with
the Virgin and Christ. Akin as these are to the
foregoing secular lullaby in poetical spirit and
philosophic outlook, they nevertheless exert a more

3

searching appeal and breathe a new atmosphere peculiarly their own. Both, obviously, arise from their religious content, but on a first reading it is a little difficult to characterise the one at all clearly and to trace the other at all convincingly to any distinctive source. The solution of the double difficulty is, I believe, to be found in the words with which Coleridge, in his *Biographia Literaria*, prefaces a verse rendering of the Nativity passage in the *Evangelienbuch*, (*c.* 870 A.D.) of the Old-Saxon poet Otfrid, or Ottfried. He says :

> 'There is a flow and a tender enthusiasm in the following lines which even in the translation will not, I flatter myself, fail to interest the reader. Ottfried is describing the circumstances immediately following the birth of our Lord. Most interesting is it to consider the effect when the feelings are wrought above the natural pitch by the belief of something mysterious, while all the images are purely natural. Then it is that religion and poetry strike deepest.'

Few incidents in history are more fraught with mystery, few more natural in their setting and circumstances, than that of the Nativity, wherein the Christ-Child, divinely conceived of the Spirit but humanly born of the flesh, is rocked upon its Virgin-Mother's knee and humbly laid to rest in a manger between ox and ass. The testimony of all branches of Christian art proves the truth of Coleridge's remark that in the treatment of such a subject religion and poetry strike deepest. The Nativity scene called forth the best both of reverence and of simple human kindliness from the composers of the liturgy, from the sculptors who adorned the cathedrals of the Middle Ages, from the writers of the medieval mystery plays, from the early

4

Renaissance artists who delighted to celebrate the Madonna and the Child, and, last but not least for our purpose, from the English writers who from the fourteenth to the twentieth century have borne witness to its inherent poetry and more than common power of inspiration. The Manger of Bethlehem is the prime source of some of the best of our lullabies. The Virgin stands forth in them as the exemplar of all human mothers. And the fate of the Babe whom it was her privilege to lull has preserved and reinforced the haunting elegiac note struck in the earliest lullaby of all.

To return for a moment to Otfrid, the lines in which he describes the greatest of cradle-scenes show how, as early as the time of Charlemagne, the poetic imagination was beginning to play around the simple statement of the gospel :

> 'And she brought forth her firstborn son, and wrapped him in swaddling clothes, and laid him in a manger ; because there was no room for them in the inn.' (*Luke* ii, 7.)

Otfrid dwells lovingly on the picture suggested. While he does not forget the mystery of the Virgin-birth, all his stress is laid upon the human element in the relations between Mother and Child. Particularly interesting are the lines, as translated by Coleridge :

> 'And blessed, blessed was the mother
> Who wrapp'd his limbs in swaddling clothes,
> Singing placed him on her lap,
> Hung o'er him with her looks of love,
> And sooth'd him with a lulling motion.'

With the flourishing of the Middle English vernacular lyric our poets develop the same conception. One or two treat the manger-scene descriptively, as

5

Otfrid does, but others freely imagine the very
words which the Virgin sang. These may vary in
substance from a simple lulling refrain to a fully
developed lament for her Child's impending earthly
fate—a fate from which, undeserved though it be,
there is, as the Mother prophetically knows, no
prospect of escape. Indeed, its fulfilment is a
necessary preliminary to her Son's final triumph,
and from this fact she derives such consolation as she
can :

> ' For love of man it mot be
>    The to suffren wo,
> For bet it is thu suffrë this
> Than man forberë hevenë blis—
>    Thu most him biyen therto.'

Meanwhile it is her task to protect him as well as
may be in such surroundings as the inn stable from
the bitter cold of the Nativity morning, to soothe
him with her human love and motherly tenderness :

> ' Ihesu, suetë sonë dere,
>    In porful bed thu list nou here,
>       And that me grevet sore ;
> ، For thi credel is als a bere,
>    Ox and Assë ben thi fere—
>       Wepen may I therfore.
>
> Ihesu, suetë, be nout wroth,
> I have neither clut ne cloth
>    The inne for to folde ;
> I ne have but a clut of a lappe,
> Therfore ley thi feet to my pappe,
>    And kep the fro the colde.'

By a typically naïve medieval licence, extended
at times to the sphere of art, the Christ-Child is
endowed even at birth with the adult faculties of

6

speech, reasoning and prophecy. Consequently the religious cradle-song of this period frequently takes the form of a dialogue between Mary and the Babe, while occasionally it develops, after an introductory stanza or two, into a monologue addressed by the prescient Babe to his despairing Mother. Of the dialogues No. IV is a beautiful example, typical of its class in its naïvety of emotion and unaffected simplicity of diction, but unique in the serenity of its atmosphere consequent upon the limitation of the argument to the happy incidents immediately following the Nativity, such as the exchange of human endearments between Mother and Son and the anticipated adoration of the Three Kings. In the majority the elegiac note predominates, harmonising with the usual theme of the Passion to come. Christ himself suggests this subject in one such dialogue :

'Sing nou, moder,' seide that child,
'Wat me sal befalle
Hereafter wan I cum to eld—
So don modres alle.

Ich a moder treuly
That kan hire credel kepe
Is wone to lullen lovely
And singgen hire child o slepe.

Swetë moder, fair and fre,
Sithen that it is so,
I preye the that thu lullë me
And sing sumwat therto.' (1)

Similar features appear in the monologues spoken by the Child. Since these are scarcely pure lullabies I have not represented them in the text, but their nature may be appreciated from the following stanzas taken from a fifteenth-century

7

example in which Christ plaintively foretells, in a tone of mingled self-pity and resignation, the tortures of the Redemption :

'Dole it is to se, her shall I be
    Hangèd upon the rode,
With baleis to-bete, my woundes to-wete,
    And geffe my fleshe to bote.

Her shal I be hangèd on a tre,
    And dye as it is skyll ;
That I have bought lesse wyll I nought ;
    It is my fader's wyll.

A spere so scharp shall perse my herte,
    For dedys that I have done.
Fader of grace, wher thou hase
    Forgetyn thy lytyll sonne ? '   (2)

Not the least attractive feature of these medieval cradle-songs is the refrain usually introduced into them. The poem last quoted, for instance, provides a charming example :

'Lullay, my chyld, and wepe no more,
    Slepe and be now still ;
The kyng of blys thi fader is,
    As it was hys wyll.'

This, besides augmenting the musical quality of the whole lyric, serves to remind us that the child of the opening stanza remains, in spite of his omniscience and gift of prophecy, a child throughout. Incidentally, also, it tends to modify the monologue in the direction of dialogue since it is intended to be sung by the Virgin. The secret of

*rode*, cross.          *baleis*, scourges.          *to-bete*, beaten.
*to-wete*, moistened.          *skyll*, reason.          *lesse*, lose, forsake.
*wher*, whether.

the apt refrain is caught again in a fifteenth-century lyric, descriptive of the Nativity, beginning :

> ' I saw a fayr maydyn
>     Syttyn and synge,
> Sche lullyd a lytyl chyld,
>     A swetë lordyng.'

' Lullay, myn lykyng, my dere sone, myn swetyng ;
Lullay, my dere herte, myn owyn dere derlyng.' (3)

In yet another the simple refrain is sung by the Babe himself with fascinating effect :

> ' Modyr, whyt as lyly flowr,
>     Yowr lullyng lessyth my langour.' (4)

The Middle English poet realised that the lullaby is essentially a lyric to be sung, and his instinctive feeling for the harmony of metre and matter never failed to suggest the prosodic form most appropriate to the particular mood to which his subject had moved him.

The fourteenth and fifteenth centuries were the golden age of the religious lullaby in England. In that period men were not afraid to acknowledge freely the simple interest which all must feel in any cradle-scene, and more particularly in the divine one, with its mystery and symbolical significance. Moreover, they were less oppressed than many of their successors in post-Reformation times by the *divinity* of the Holy Family. For them Mary and Christ were primarily Mother and Child, with the simple emotions of all human mothers and children. To these emotions the poets gave the most fitting utterance, most fitting because most natural, and most natural because most near to the language and imagery that mothers are accustomed to use in singing to their children. Their attitude to-

9

wards the Virgin and the Babe is one of intimacy,
intimacy without the slightest suspicion of irrever-
ence.   It is the attitude of the medieval dramatists,
exemplified in the Nativity scene of the Towneley
*Second Shepherds' Play* (5), where the three shepherds,
greeting the Child in the manger, present gifts not
prophetic or symbolical, as the gold, frankincense
and myrrh of the Magi, but in keeping with their
rustic nature and Christ's human babyhood.   The
lyrical speeches with which they accompany their
gifts are well-known, but I cannot resist quoting
from them.   Owing, as they do, nothing to any
suggestion in the gospels, they convey most naturally
and spontaneously the true feelings of their age.
The First Shepherd, offering a bob of cherries,
says :

> ' Lo, he laghys, my swetyng,
>     A welfare metyng,
>     I have holden my hetyng ;
>         Have a bob of cherys.'

The Second Shepherd presents a bird :

> 'A byrd have I broght
>     To my barne.
> Hayll, lytyll tynë mop !
> Of oure crede thou art crop :
> I wold drynk on thy cop,
>     Lytyll day starne.'

And the Third Shepherd gives a tennis-ball :

> ' Hayll !   Put furth thy dall !
> I bryng the bot a ball :
> Have and play thee with all,
>     And go to the tenys ! '

| | | |
|---|---|---|
| *hetyng*, promise. | *barne*, bairn, child. | *mop*, baby. |
| *crop*, head. | *cop*, cup. | *starne*, star. |
| *dall*, hand. | | |

Such things were possible in poetry and drama when religion and the muses walked hand in hand, but they were more difficult after the Reformation. Subsequent Virgin lullabies (and a striking feature of the English lullaby is the permanence of the Virgin-to-her-Babe tradition) tend to become more deferential, if the word may be permitted in such a connection, more impersonal, more historical, or more abstract in their philosophy. They are frequently beautiful, but with few exceptions their beauty is rather different in kind.

With the renaissance of song in the latter half of the sixteenth century the lullaby enjoyed a renewed popularity, but it is no longer the lullaby of the earlier period. Although the medieval note of elegy persists in many of the sleep songs of the Elizabethan, Jacobean and Caroline era, they show a greater variety of theme, due largely to the fact that the majority are non-religious in import. Relatively few of these secular lullabies are concerned with children. In such as are, however, the function of the mother, or it might be the nurse, is still to console. Not pervasively now, but frequently enought to determine the atmosphere, the philosophy of *Lollai, lollai, litil child* finds utterance, perhaps in a half-hearted hope that ' dolours ' will ' be fleeting,' perhaps in an elegiac refrain, such as that of Robert Greene's *Sephestia's Lullaby* (xii) :

' Weep not, my wanton, smile upon my knee,
  When thou art old there's grief enough for thee.'

Greene's Sephestia, however, unlike the mother of the medieval lullaby, is less concerned with anticipation of the child's future than with recollections of the father's sad parting from them both :

'The wanton smiled, father wept,
    Mother cried, baby leapt ;
More he crowed, more we cried,
    Nature could not sorrow hide :
He must go, he must kiss
    Child and mother, baby bliss,
For he left his pretty boy,
    Father's sorrow, father's joy.'

In two or three others, such as *Balow* (xiii) and *Come, little babe, come, silly soul* (xiv), the sorrow of separation is intensified by the fact that the babe is the emblem of the ' father's shame,' the ' mother's grief.' The love that the mother cannot help cherishing for the father who has deserted her finds expression in increased tenderness towards her one ' comfort and joy,' the innocent pledge of a passion by which ' she purchased blame.'

In the greater number of the secular lullabies of this period, more especially in those taken from the Jacobean and Caroline dramatists, the object to be lulled is not a child. Usually it is a mistress (*e.g.* viii, xviii, xxi, xxx, xxxiv) ; occasionally it is a sick or sorrowing king (*e.g.* xx, xxxiii), queen (*e.g.* xxiii) or lover (*e.g.* xxvi); in the inimitable song from *A Midsummer Night's Dream* (xv) it is Titania, the Queen of Faery ; while in a few instances, such as *Gascoigne's Lullaby* for his youthful wanton impulses (vii), Sir Philip Sidney's *Sleep, baby mine, Desire !* (ix) and the anonymous *Sleep, sleep, my soul* (xxv), it is some conceit of the poet's fancy. These extensions of the sphere of the lullaby were almost to be expected in such an age. If justification for my admission of the resulting poems to the present anthology be demanded, it is to be found in the double fact that they conform to the normal conventions of the lullaby, even if they are not intended to be sung over the cradle of a child (for there is nothing in either the dictionary's definition or the general interpretation of the word 'lullaby' to limit its application to cradle-songs), and that, with few exceptions, they are suffused with the song-like quality and subdued elegiac atmosphere so characteristic of the majority of English lullabies.

In sheer poetical beauty these songs often vie with the best lyrics of their age, which is merely another way of saying that they are among the finest short lyrics in the language. Could anything, for instance, be more delicate and graceful, in spite of its touch of conceit, than the anonymous *Weep you no more, sad fountains* (XVIII), with its exquisite second stanza ?—

> ' Sleep is a reconciling,
>  A rest that peace begets ;
> Doth not the sun rise smiling
>  When fair at even he sets ?
> Rest you then, rest, sad eyes !
>  Melt not in weeping,
>  While she lies sleeping
> Softly, now softly lies
>  Sleeping.'

Or, again, could anything be more perfect in sentiment and expression than the following anonymous lines (XXXV) sung over one who is seeking relief from sickness in a few moments of restless slumber ?—

' She sleeps. Peace crown thine eyes ! Sweet dreams in deep,
Softest security thy senses steep !
Aye me ! she groans. Sadly, alas, oppressed
Lies the dear bosom gasping without rest.

13

Sickness, not sleep's numb hand, her eyes' faint
    ray
And those dead ashes of her cheek bewray,
Whose ominous hue (as bent t' invert our years)
Like winter's snow on April buds appears.
So the vexed morn from her sere lover's bed
And cold embraces, with a look of lead,
Pale and delightless rises ; the autumn bower
So wanes, so falling droops the evening flower,
As life this fair declining lamp of light
(Her shine contracting) all o'erhaled in night.'

The fact that both of these songs are anonymous,
while several others of as high a lyrical quality come
from quite minor authors, is only to be explained
by reference to the lyrical fertility of the age
generally. It was pre-eminently an age of singers,
when nearly every humble versifier succeeded at
some happy moment in his variable poetic career
in approaching the heights which only the greatest
could maintain at all consistently. For us it is
fortunate that several reached their zenith in their
songs of lullaby.

The religious lullabies of the time are less poetical
in spirit and very much fewer in number than the
secular. Of the four given in the text three are
concerned with the Virgin and the Child. Not one
of these, however, can compare favourably either
with the current secular lullabies or with the
medieval Virgin lullabies. *The Virgin's Song* (xxii)
from John Attey's *First Book of Airs* (1622) has a
touch of the old-time freshness and charm, but there
is an appreciable falling-off in quality in *Be still,
my blessed Babe* (x), a rather uninspired treatment
in the jog-trot Poulter's measure of the Virgin's
attitude towards the Slaughter of the Innocents and
the Flight into Egypt, and also in Richard Row-

lands' *Our Blessed Lady's Lullaby*, which, apart from the first four stanzas included as XVII, is rather barren both of tender feeling and of poetry.

The remaining religious lullaby of the four, George Wither's *Rocking Hymn* (XXXII), is, as the prefatory note reveals, inspired by a new purpose :

> ' Nurses usually sing their Children asleep ; and through want of pertinent matter, they oft make use of unprofitable (if not worse) Songs. This was therefore prepared, that it might help acquaint them, and their Nurse-Children, with the loving Care and Kindnesse of their heavenly Father.'

The result is unfortunate. Wither might well have added the quotation which had appeared four years previously on the title-page of Milton's *Comus* (1637)—

> ' Eheu quod volui misero mihi ! floribus austrum
> Perditus '—

for in his tasteless insistence on conception in sin and in the manner of his elaboration of God's goodness to the average human child, whose comfortable surroundings are contrasted with the cold Manger of Bethlehem, one sees the numbing influence of Puritanism. The purely verbal charm of the poem is marred by the chilly, depreciatory atmosphere which this new influence induces. Wither's second *Rocking Hymn*, which I have not included, is steeped in this atmosphere to its complete undoing. Only a disarming simplicity, a touch of the quality that won immense popularity for *O God, our help in ages past* and other of his hymns, saves from a like fate the *Cradle Hymn* (XXXIX) written by the Nonconformist Isaac Watts in the early years of the next century. In short, amenable though the lullaby be to the purposes of true elegy, it proves restive when saddled with the task of conveying to unthinking children religious consolation of the rather grudging Genevan variety.

Apart from Philip Ayres' poem *On a Child sleeping in Cynthia's Lap* (xxxviii), this *Cradle Hymn* of Watts is the only lullaby for a child that I have found in the century and a half elapsing between the appearance of Wither's *Haleluiah* (1641) and the publication of William Blake's *Songs of Innocence* (1789). Indeed the whole field of the lullaby, whether for child or adult, is unusually barren in this period. This is not surprising, for, after all, one would scarcely expect an outburst of lullaby-writing from the Rochesters and Sedleys of the Restoration or from the Popes of the Augustan age. Naïvety, enthusiasm, tenderness, these and such other emotional qualities as the lullaby thrives upon, were all too effectively repressed, in literature at least, by the sophisticated intellectualism of the periods in question. Only with the Romantic Revival of the end of the eighteenth century did they emerge once more, and their reappearance was immediately followed by a renewed activity in the sphere of the lullaby.

The spirit of romanticism engendered a keen interest in childhood in several of the poets of the late eighteenth and early nineteenth centuries, more particularly in Blake and Wordsworth. No man was ever better qualified to sing of children than Blake, for the simple reason that he never ceased to be a child himself; of such as he is the Kingdom of Heaven. A mystic, the essence of his mysticism lies in the fact that he saw the world through the eyes of childhood, saw it as it really was beneath the distorting haze of man-inspired materialism. Moreover, he saw that it was good. To his joy in the discovery he gave voice with the naturalness and spontaneity of a child. Throughout his *Songs of Innocence*, indeed, he is just the supremely articulate child speaking for his less articulate fellow-children.

In the *Cradle Song* (XLII) from the *Songs of Innocence* Blake reveals his sympathetic insight through the pure music of a mother's crooning, in lines where sound vies with sense for pride of place :

> 'Sweet dreams, form a shade
> O'er my lovely infant's head ;
> Sweet dreams of pleasant streams
> By happy, silent, moony beams.'

The mother's task is to soothe, not to shatter the dreams of Innocence by voicing the forebodings of Experience. Even if she weep, her child must smile. Christ in his cradle once wept for them both, so that he might leave to his heirs a legacy of smiles :

> 'Infant smiles are His own smiles ;
> Heaven and earth to peace beguiles.'

But the poet who wrote the *Songs of Innocence* wrote also the *Songs of Experience*. Blake regretted Experience, not because it necessarily involved sorrow and misfortune, but because it severed precious links with childlike simplicity and guilelessness, and these, once broken, could never be restored. His second *Cradle Song* (XLIII), intended, no doubt, for the *Songs of Experience* although never included amongst them, well illustrates this. Night, or Experience, casting its shadow before it over a sleeping baby-girl, fills her with dreams of her future charms. Maturity will perfect the pretty wiles of infancy into instruments of conquest :

'O ! the cunning wiles that creep
In thy little heart asleep.
When thy little heart does wake
Then the dreadful lightnings break,

From thy cheek and from thy eye,
O'er the youthful harvests nigh.
Infant wiles and infant smiles
Heaven and Earth of peace beguiles.'

The infant smiles of Innocence had beguiled Heaven and Earth *to* peace ; those of Experience beguile them *of* it. And that, for Blake, is the pity of it.

Wordsworth also regretted adolescence, because, as he viewed it, its successive stages are marked by a progressive weakening of the ties that connect us with the heaven that ' lies about us in our infancy.' He differs from Blake in so far as his bent of mind leads him to contemplate childhood as an abstract philosophic state rather than as a passing phase in the development of individual children. Consequently he never relaxes to lulling song. One suspects, indeed, that in the eyes of the author of the Ode on *Intimations of Immortality from Recollections of Early Childhood* the babe—' Thou best philosopher,' ' Mighty prophet ! seer blest ! ' and so on —is far too solemnly and securely invested with the aura of immortality to feel the need of any human soothing. But Burns, Coleridge, Scott and Keats, and the lesser-known Gall, Kirke White and Hogg felt the attraction of the cradle-song. Their efforts, brief as they are for the most part, serve to prove that the adoption of a conventional poetical form does not necessarily involve the adoption of a set of stereotyped emotions and images. On the contrary, the characteristic tastes of these individual authors appear clearly in their lullabies. The playful humour of *The Highland Balou* (XLIV), for instance, stamps it as the work of Burns. The martial note of *The Lullaby of an Infant Chief* (LI) reveals the hand of the poet of *Marmion* and *The Lady of the Lake*. To those who know the tastes of the youthful Kirke White his authorship of the rather morbid but nevertheless affecting *Lullaby of a Female Convict to her Child, the Night previous to Execution* (XLVI) will come as no surprise, while Hogg's two cradle songs (XLVIII, LIV), in which an unhappy spectre and a dying mother look forward to reunion with their babes

' In valleys beyond the land of the dew,'

are recognised as being very typical of their author. Richard Gall, an almost forgotten contemporary and friend of Burns, charmingly illustrates the wistful tenderness and disarming simplicity of the Scots verse of his time in his tuneful lullaby for a child (XLV) whose

' daddy now is far awa',
A sailor laddie o'er the sea,'

where, as in the songs of Scott, Kirke White and Hogg, the familiar undertones of elegiac lament are heard once more.

The second quarter of the nineteenth century saw a development that might well have proved a turning-point in the history of the lullaby. This was the entry of women writers into the field. The fact is, however, that their lullabies mark no very striking innovations either in form or idea on those of their male predecessors. Perhaps this is to be construed as a tribute to the sympathetic insight of the latter ; more probably it is only an instance of the timidity of the pioneer female writers in departing from established literary usages, of their

19

desire to meet men on their own ground rather than venture along more congenial paths of their own making :

' Today if any lady in her boudoir rhymeth,
  She is drown'd in man's tradition and disguiseth
      her tone,
Transposing her high music to the lower clef.' (6)

True, the distinctively feminine touch is felt occasionally, as, for instance, in Sara Coleridge's stanza (LII) :

' A thousand infant faces, soft and sweet,
  Each year sends forth, yet every mother views
        Her last not least beloved
        Like its dear self alone ' ;

and again in Elizabeth Barrett Browning's conception of the Virgin's natural disappointment because her Babe is ' A child, without the heart for play ' :

' Unchildlike shade !—No other babe doth wear
  An aspect very sorrowful, as Thou.—
  No small babe-smiles, my watching heart has seen,
  To float like speech the speechless lips between :
  No dovelike cooing in the golden air,
  No quick short joys of leaping babyhood.
        Alas, our earthly good
  In heaven thought evil, seems too good for Thee :
        Yet, sleep, my weary One ! '

But in no single instance is one forced to say, ' Here is a lullaby which could have been written *only* by a woman.' Not even of Mrs. Browning's long and well-sustained monologue of *The Virgin Mary to the Child Jesus* (LIII) can this assertion be made, yet this is easily the most impressive lullaby of any woman writer. Her analysis of the conflicting hopes and fears of the Virgin is convincing. Why, the Virgin asks, should she, who

> ' often wandered forth, more child than maiden,
> Among the midnight hills of Galilee
>     Whose summits looked heaven-laden,
> Listening to silence as it seemed to be
> God's voice, so soft yet strong '—

why should she have been hailed as ' the blessedest of women ' ? Why from her corruption should the Incorruptible have sprung ? But if the past is shrouded in mystery, the future is at times made all too clear by ' the drear sharp tongue of prophecy ' :

>        ' Then, I think aloud
> The words " despised,"—" rejected,"—every word
> Recoiling into darkness as I view
>     The DARLING on my knee.
> Bright angels,—move not !—lest ye stir the cloud
> Betwixt my soul and His futurity !
> I must not die, with mother's work to do,
>     And could not live—and see.'

These last two lines present the Virgin's dilemma perfectly.

It is unfortunate that other women writers not represented here should have failed to enrich the literature of lullabies either emotionally or poetically ; and it is even more unfortunate that they should agree in showing a tendency towards sentimentality when treating of children that prevents them from doing justice even to such poetical ability as they show elsewhere.

Among the poets of the middle and late nineteenth century who favour the lullaby Tennyson

(LVIII, LIX), Clough (LX), and Christina Rossetti (LXI) strike a lighter note and attempt a simpler and more childish diction than the majority of their forerunners had done. Their cradle songs are genuinely young children's, if not babies', poems. The same might have been said of Barnes' *Lullaby* (LXII) had not the dialect in which it is written made it difficult of comprehension to children not born in rural Dorset. Swinburne also, the Swinburne whom Mr. Robert Graves, one of his victims, describes as an inveterate baby patter and kisser, restricts himself to the simplest of words and thoughts in such poems of childhood as *A Baby's Death*, *Etude Réaliste*, and *Babyhood*, three sequences from *A Century of Roundels* (1883), and in the series of seven *Cradle Songs* included in the present collection (LXIII). These charming *Cradle Songs* are, as Swinburne says, set ' to a tune of Blake's,'—obviously that of *Silent, silent Night* in the Rossetti MS. But Swinburne does more than borrow the metre of his songs from Blake ; he endeavours to appreciate and reproduce the older poet's spiritual outlook on childhood. To a certain extent, he succeeds. The fourth *Cradle Song* of his sequence, for instance, in which he expresses his belief in the security of innocent babyhood against the guile and falsehood of man, is very much in the spirit of Blake. Its last stanza would probably have won the approval of Wordsworth as well :

> ' Man, a dunce uncouth,
> Errs in age and youth :
> Babies know the truth.'

Similarly, I fancy, but in a much higher degree, has Mr. Yeats grasped the quintessential genius of the *Songs of Innocence* and distilled some drop of it into

the *Cradle Song* of his with which this anthology
concludes (LXV). This, surely, is as perfect an
example of lullaby poetry as transparent emotion,
mystical insight, Gaelic other-worldliness and severe
simplicity of diction could combine to produce.
And the mother's cry of the last two lines—

> ' Ah, how I shall miss you
> When you have grown ! '—

vibrates in sympathy with the elegiac note which
has sounded, now dimly, now clearly, through six
centuries of English lullabies.

Naturally the cradle-song is not peculiar to
English poetry. The instinct to croon in rhythmic
harmony with the rocking of the cradle is, no doubt,
as old as motherhood and as universal, and the
evidence of those literatures whose immature stages
are represented by extant popular song shows that
the cradle-scene readily kindled the unsophisticated
imagination of poets accustomed to celebrate the
familiar scenes of everyday life. Their primitive
lullabies are marked by absolute simplicity both of
rhythm and substance ; the rhythm, indeed, being
determined by the necessity of imitating in word
and music the mother's lulling motion, scarcely
varies, whatever the language. So long as the
lullaby was, as in these early stages, genuinely intended for mothers to sing to young children, it
shared the nature of nursery-rhyme poetry. This
was inevitable, for the limits of childish comprehension are narrow. Only when the cradle-scene came
to be treated conventionally, when the mother was
made the mouthpiece not of her own so much as of
the poet's reflections and her auditor was no longer
really the babe but rather the adult reader, only
then did the fully articulated lullaby, as we have it
in the present anthology, evolve.

23

The conventional lullaby is considerably less common in foreign literatures than the nursery-rhyme type. When it does occur, it is generally, as in France, a late product designed to meet the special taste of Romanticism for studied simplicity. In England, however, as this brief survey will have shown, it had long before matured and had flourished abundantly, particularly during the late Middle Ages and the popular Renaissance of the end of the sixteenth and the beginning of the seventeenth century, those two periods of our poetry when emotion found utterance most simply and most spontaneously through conventional lyric forms. That we alone should enjoy a lullaby literature extending over some six centuries, high in poetical quality, continuous in tradition, and wide in appeal, is a striking fact, and one that invites explanation. In my opinion, as I have already suggested, the reason is to be sought in the fact that the English lullaby was from its very inception marked by the high seriousness that is the predominating feature of the national literary genius. To the Middle English poet the cradle-scene, wherein Experience is placed in the most intimate contact with weeping Innocence, offered an opportunity for elegiac reflection that was too favourable to be foregone. His approach to it was, from the first, wholly conventional, as his particular concern with the manger-scene of Bethlehem shows. By writing lullabies for the Virgin's lips he automatically renounced any realistic or utilitarian purpose, and gave himself up instead to the free indulgence of his taste for contemplating the most human scenes from the gospels of his adopted religion through the darkening medium of his innate pagan melancholy. The English lullaby was, therefore, born into kinship with elegy, and this relationship has never since been wholly obscured. The elegy reflects one of the most characteristic aspects of the racial temperament, and there can, I think, be no doubt that it is precisely to its elegiac affinities that the English lullaby owes its unique virility and permanence.

# I

### *Lollai, Lollai, Litil Child*

LOLLAI, lollai, litil child,
　　Whi wepistou so sore ?
Nedis mostou wepe,
　　Hit was iyarkid the yore
Ever to lib in sorow,
　　And sich and mourne evere,
As thin eldren did er this,
　　Whil hi alivës were.
　　　　　　Lollai, lollai, litil child,
　　　　　　　　Child, lolai, lullow !
　　　　　　Into uncuth world
　　　　　　　　Icommen so ertow.

Bestis and thos foulës,
　　The fisses in the flode,
And euch schef alivës,
　　Imakid of bone and blode,
Whan hi commith to the world
　　Hi doth ham silf sum gode—
Al bot the wrech brol
　　That is of Adamis blode.
　　　　　　Lollai, lollai, litil child !
　　　　　　　　To kar ertou bemette ;
　　　　　　Thou nost noght this worldis wild
　　　　　　　　Bifor the is isette.

Child, if it betidith
　　That thou ssalt thrive and the,

4. *iyarkid*, prepared, ordained.　　6. *sich*, sigh.
11. *uncuth*, unknown.　　15. *schef*, creature.
19. *brol*, child.　　22. *bemette*, adjudged.
25. *it*, not in MS.　　26. *the*, prosper.

Thench thou wer ifostred
   Up thi moder kne ;
Ever hab mund in thi hert
   Of thos thingës thre,
Whan thou commist, whan thou art,
   And what ssal com of the.
          Lollai, lollai, litil child,
            Child, lollai, lollai !
          With sorow thou com into this world,
          With sorow ssalt wend awai.

Ne tristou to this world ;
   Hit is thi ful vo.
The rich he makith pouer,
   The porë rich also.
Hit turneth wo to wel,
   And ekë wel to wo—
Ne trist no man to this world,
   Whil hit turnith so.
          Lollai, lollai, litil child !
            The fote is in the whele.
         Thou nost whoder turne
          To wo other wele.

Child, thou ert a pilgrim
   In wikidnis ibor ;
Thou wandrest in this fals world,
   Thou lokë the bifor.
Deth ssal com with a blast
   Ute of a wel dim horre,
Adamis kin dun to cast,
   Him silf hath ido befor.
         Lollai, lollai, litil child !
         So wo the worp Adam

29. *mund*, memory.        31. *whan*, whence.
38. *vo*, foe.           47. *whoder*, whether.
54. *wel dim horre*, very obscure door (or fog).
58. *worp*, wove, prepared (Carleton Brown's emendation for MS. *worþ*, worth).

In the lond of Paradis
Throgh wikidnes of Satan.

Child, thou nert a pilgrim,
Bot an uncuthe gist ;
Thi dawës beth itold,
Thi iurneis beth icast.
Whoder thou salt wend,
North other est,
Deth the sal betide
With bitter bale in brest.
Lollai, lollai, litil child !
This wo Adam the wroght,
Whan he of the appil ete,
And Eve hit him betacht.

ANONYMOUS

*MS. British Museum, Harley 913, c.* 1308-1318.

62. *gist*, guest.
64. *icast*, forecast.

63. *dawës*, days ; *itold*, reckoned.
72. *betacht*, gave.

## II

*A Lullaby to Christ in the Cradle*

LULLAY, lullay, litel child !
  Child, reste the a throwe ;
Fro heyghe hider art thu sent
  With us to wonë lowe ;
Pore and litel art thu mad,
  Unkut and unknowe,
Pine an wo to suffren her
  For thing that was thin owe.
      Lullay, lullay, litel child !
        Sorwë mauth thu make ;
      Thu art sent into this werd,
        As tu were forsake.


Lullay, lullay, litel grom,
  King of allë thingge !
Wan I thenke of thi methchef
  Me listet wol litel singge ;
But caren I may for sorwe,
  Yef love wer in myn herte,
For suichë peines as thu salt driyen
  Were nevere non so smerte.
      Lullay, lullay, litel child !
        Wel mauth thu criye,
      For than thi bodi is bleyk and blak,
        Sone after sal ben driye.

2. *throwe*, space of time.          4. *wonë*, dwell.
7. *Pine*, suffering.                10. *mauth*, mayest.
11. *werd*, world.                   13. *grom*, groom.
15. *methchef*, misfortune.          19. *driyen*, suffer.
23. *bleyk and blak*, pale and wan.  24. *driye*, lifeless.

Child, it is a weping dale
　That thu art comen inne ;
Thi pore clutes it proven wel,
　Thi bed mad in the binne ;
Cold and hunger thu must tholen
　As thu were geten in senne,
And after deyyen on the tre
　For love of al mankenne.
　　　　Lullay, lullay, litel child !
　　　　　No wonder thou thu care ;
　　　　Thu art comen amongës hem
　　　　That thi deth sulen yare.

Lullay, lullay, litel child !
　For sorwë mauth thu grete ;
The anguis that thu suffren salth
　Sal don the blod to suete ;
Naked, bunden saltu ben,
　And seithen sorë bete,
Nothing fre upon thi bodi
　Of pinë sal be lete.
　　　　Lullay, lullay, litel child !
　　　　　It is al for thi fo,
　　　　The hardë bond of love longging
　　　　That the hat bunden so.

Lullay, lullay, litel child,
　Litel child, thin ore !
It is al for oure owen gilt
　That thu art peinèd sore ;
But woldë we yet kindë be,
　And liven after thi lore,

27. *clutes*, clothes.　　　　28. *binne*, manger.
29. *tholen*, suffer.　　　　30. *geten*, begotten.
36. *sulen yare*, shall prepare.　38. *grete*, weep.
40. *don the blod to suete*, cause thee to sweat blood.
44. *lete*, left.　　　　　50. *ore*, grace, favour.

30

And leten sennë for thi love,
Ne keptest thu no more.
　　　　Lullay, lullay, litel child,
　　　　Softë slep and faste !
　　　　In sorwë endet everi love
　　　　But thin at the laste.
　　　　　　　　　　　Amen.

ANONYMOUS

MS. *Advocates Library, 18.7.21,* 1372.

56. *Ne keptest thu,* thou wouldest not care.

# III

*The Virgin's Song to her Shivering Babe*

Ler to loven as I love the ;
On al my limes thu mith i-se
 Hou sore thei quaken for colde ;
For the I suffre michil wo.
Love me, suetë, an no-mo—
 To the I take and holde.

Ihesu, suetë sonë dere,
In porful bed thu list nou here,
 And that me grevet sore ;
For thi credel is als a bere,
Ox and Assë ben thi fere—
 Wepen may I therfore.

Ihesu, suetë, be nout wroth,
I have neither clut ne cloth
 The inne for to folde ;
I ne have but a clut of a lappe,
Therfore ley thi feet to my pappe,
 And kep the fro the colde.

Cold the taket, I may wel se.
For love of man it mot be
 The to suffren wo,
For bet it is thu suffrë this
Than man forberë hevenë blis—
 Thu most him biyen therto.

1. *ler*, teach.     10. *bere*, bier.
11. *fere*, companions.   16. *lappe*, skirt.
23. *forberë*, be deprived of.   24. *biyen*, buy.

Sythen it most nedes that thu be ded
To saven man fro the qued,
    Thi suetë wil be do.
But let me nouth duellen her to longe ;
After thi det me underfonge
    To ben for everemo.
              Amen.

                    ANONYMOUS

*Ibid.*

25. *Sythen*, since.        26. *qued*, devil, or evil.
29. *underfonge*, receive.

# IV

## A Dialogue between the Blessed Virgin and Her Child

*Thys endris nyght*
*I saw a sight,*
> *A stare as bryght as day ;*
*And ever among*
*A mayden song*
> *' Lullay, by by, lullay.'*

THIS lovely lady sat and song,
  And to hyr chyld thus gan she say :
' My sone, my broder, my fader der,
  Why lyest thou thus in hay ?
    My swetë bryd
    Thus it is betyde,
      Thow thou be kyng veray ;
    But nevertheles
    I wyl not ses
      To syng, By by, lullay.'


The chyld than spak in hys talkyng,
  And to hys moder sayd,
' I am knowen as hevyn kyng
  In crybbe thowgh I be layd.
    For aungeiles bryght
    Done to me lyght,
      Thou knowest it is no nay ;
    And of that syght
    Thou mayst be lyght
      To syng, By by, lullay.'

1. *endris*, last          11. *bryd*, bird.

'Now, swet son, syn thou art kyng,
Why art thou layd in stall ?
Why ne thou ordende thi beddyng
In sum gret kyngës hall ?
Me thynkyth it is ryght,
That kyng or knyght
Shuld ly in good aray ;
And than among
It wer no wrong
To syng, By by, lullay.'

'Mary moder, I am thi chyld,
Thow I be layd in stall,
Lordes and dukes shal worsshyp me
And so shall kyngës all.
Ye shall well se
That kyngës thre
Shal come the xij day,
For this behest
Gefe me thi brest,
And syng, By by, lullay.'

'Now tell me, swet son, I the pray,
Thou art me leve and dere,
How shuld I kepe the to thy pay
And mak the glad of chere.
For all thi wyll
I wold fullfyll,
Thou wetyste full well, in fay ;
And for all thys
I wyll the kys,
And syng, By by, lullay.'

'My der moder, whan tym it be,
Thou take me up on loft,
And set me upon thi kne,
And handyll me full soft ;

49. *pay*, satisfaction.          53. *wetyste*, knowest.

35

And in thi arme
Thou hyl me warme,
   And kepë nyght and day ;
And if I wepe,
And may not slepe,
   Thou syng, By by, lullay.'

' Now, swet son, syn it is so,
   That all thyng is at thi wyll,
I pray the graunte me a bone,
   Yf it be both ryght and skyll,
   That chyld or man
   That wyl or kan
    Be mery upon my day,
To blyse hem bryng,
And I shal syng,
   Lullay, by by, lullay.'

ANONYMOUS

*MS. Bodley 29734, Eng. Poet. e. 1, c. 1460-1480.*

62. *hyl*, protect.        70. *skyll*, reason.

# V

*The Song of the Mothers to their Innocents*

*Lully, lulla, thow littell tinë child ;*
*By by, lully, lullay, thow littell tynë child ;*
*By by, lully, lullay !*

O SISTERS too,
How may we do
        For to preserve this day
This pore yongling
For whom we do singe
        By by, lully, lullay ?

Herod, the king,
In his raging,
        Chargid he hath this day
His men of might
In his owne sight
        All yonge children to slay,—

That wo is me,
Pore child, for thee,
        And ever morne and may
For thi parting
Neither say nor singe,
        By by, lully, lullay.

**ANONYMOUS**

From *The Pageant of the Shearmen and Taylors*, a XVth Century
Coventry Corpus Christi Play ; MS., 1534.

18. *may,* Kittredge's emendation for MS. *say.*

# VI

## *The Nurse's Song*

*Lullaby baby, lullaby baby,*
*Thy nurse will tend thee as duly as may be.*

BE still, my sweet sweeting, no longer do cry ;
　Sing lullaby baby, lullaby baby.
Let dolours be fleeting, I fancy thee, I,
　To rock and to lull thee I will not delay me.
　　Lullaby baby, lullaby baby,
　　Thy nurse will tend thee as duly as may be.

What creature now living would hasten thy woe ?
　Sing lullaby, lullaby, lullaby baby.
See for thy relieving the time I bestow,
　To dance and to prance thee as prettily as may be.
　　Lullaby baby, lullaby baby,
　　Thy nurse will tend thee as duly as may be.

The gods be thy shield and comfort in need !
　Sing lullaby, lullaby, lullaby baby.
They give thee good fortune and well for to speed,
　And this to desire I will not delay me.
　　Lullaby baby, lullaby baby,
　　Thy nurse will tend thee as duly as may be.

JOHN PHILLIP
*fl. 1566-1591*

*The Play of Patient Grissell, Stationers' Register,* 1565-6, 1568-9.

# VII

*Gascoigne's Lullaby*

SING lullaby, as women do,
    Wherewith they bring their babes to rest ;
And lullaby can I sing too,
    As womanly as can the best.
With lullaby they still the child ;
And if I be not much beguiled,
Full many a wanton babe have I,
Which must be still'd with lullaby.

First lullaby my youthful years,
    It is now time to go to bed :
For crookèd age and hoary hairs
    Have won the haven within my head.
With lullaby, then, youth be still ;
With lullaby content thy will ;
Since courage quails and comes behind,
Go sleep, and so beguile thy mind !

Next lullaby my gazing eyes,
    Which wonted were to glance apace ;
For every glass may now suffice
    To show the furrows in thy face.
With lullaby then wink awhile ;
With lullaby your looks beguile ;
Let no fair face, nor beauty bright,
Entice you eft with vain delight.

And lullaby my wanton will ;
    Let reason's rule now reign thy thought ;
Since all too late I find by skill
    How dear I have thy fancies bought ;

With lullaby now take thine ease,
With lullaby thy doubts appease ;
For trust to this, if thou be still,
My body shall obey thy will.

Thus lullaby my youth, mine eyes,
 My will, my ware, and all that was :
I can no more delays devise ;
 But welcome pain, let pleasure pass.
With lullaby now take your leave ;
With lullaby your dreams deceive ;
And when you rise with waking eye,
Remember then this lullaby.

GEORGE GASCOIGNE
*1525 ?-1577*

*A Hundred Sundry Flowers*, 1573.

# VIII

## *Musidorus' Lullaby for Pamela*

Lock up, fair lids, the treasure of my heart ;
Preserve those beams, this age's only light ;
To her sweet sense, sweet sleep, some ease impart,
Her sense too weak to bear her spirit's might.
And while, O sleep, thou closest up her sight,
(Her sight where love did forge his fairest dart)
O harbour all her parts in easeful plight ;
Let no strange dream make her fair body start.
But yet, O dream, if thou wilt not depart
In this rare subject from the common right,
But wilt thyself in such a seat delight,
Then take my shape and play a lover's part :
Kiss her from me, and say unto her sprite,
Till her eyes shine, I live in darkest night.

SIR PHILIP SIDNEY
*1554-1586*

*Arcadia, Lib. 3,* 1593.   Before 1586.

# IX

### *Sleep, Baby Mine, Desire!*

'Sleep, baby mine, Desire!' Nurse Beauty
    singeth.
'Thy cries, O baby, set mine head on aching.'
The babe cries 'Way, thy love doth keep me
    waking.'

'Lully, lully, my babe! Hope cradle bringeth
Unto my children always good rest taking.'
The babe cries 'Way, thy love doth me keep
    waking.'

'Since, baby mine, from me, thy watching
    springeth,
Sleep then a little ; pap Content is making' :
The babe cries 'Nay! for that abide I waking.'

SIR PHILIP SIDNEY

From *Certain Sonnets* in the *Folio* of 1598. Before 1586.

# X

## *Be Still, my Blessed Babe*

*Lulla la, lullaby !*
*My sweet little Baby,*
*What meanest thou to cry ?*

Be still, my blessed Babe, though cause thou hast
to mourn,
Whose blood most innocent to shed the cruel king
hath sworn ;
And lo, alas, behold, what slaughter he doth make,
Shedding the blood of infants all, sweet Saviour,
for Thy sake !
A King is born, they say, which King this king
would kill.
O woe, and woeful heavy day, when wretches have
their will !

*Lulla la, lullaby !*
*My sweet little Baby,*
*What meanest thou to cry ?*

Three kings this King of kings to see are come from
far,
To each unknown, with offerings great, by guiding
of a star :
And shepherds heard the song which Angels bright
did sing,
Giving all glory unto God for coming of this King,
Which must be made away, king Herod would
him kill.
O woe, and woeful heavy day, when wretches have
their will !

*Lulla la, lullaby !*
*My sweet little Baby,*
*What meanest thou to cry ?*

Lo, lo, my little Babe, be still, lament no more !
From fury thou shalt step aside, help have we still
    in store.
We heavenly warning have some other soil to seek,
From death must fly the Lord of life, as Lamb both
    mild and meek.
Thus must my Babe obey the king that would him
    kill.
O woe, and woeful heavy day, when wretches have
    their will !

*Lulla la, lullaby !*
*My sweet little Baby,*
*What meanest thou to cry ?*

But thou shalt live and reign as Sibyls have foresaid,
As all the Prophets prophesy ; whose Mother, yet
    a Maid
And perfect Virgin pure, with her breasts shall
    upbreed
Both God and man, that all hath made, the Son
    of heavenly seed :
Whom caitiffs none can 'tray, whom tyrants none
    can kill.
O joy, and joyful happy day, when wretches want
    their will !

ANONYMOUS

William Byrd's *Psalms, Sonnets and Songs of Sadness and Piety*,
  1588.

# XI

## *Sleep! Sleep! Mine only Jewel*

SLEEP ! Sleep ! mine only jewel ;
Much more thou didst delight me,
Than my beloved, too cruel,
That hid her face to spite me.

Thou bring'st her home full nigh me
    While she so fast did fly me.
By thy means I behold those eyes so shining,
Long time absented, that look so mild appeased.
    Thus is my grief declining ;
Thou, in thy dreams, dost make desire well pleased.
Sleep ! if thou be like death, as thou art feigned,
A happy life by such a death were gained.

ANONYMOUS

Nicholas Yonge's *Musica Transalpina*, 1588.

# XII

## *Sephestia's Lullaby*

WEEP not, my wanton, smile upon my knee ;
When thou art old there's grief enough for thee.
    Mother's wag, pretty boy,
    Father's sorrow, father's joy ;
    When thy father first did see
    Such a boy by him and me,
    He was glad, I was woe ;
    Fortune changèd made him so,
    When he left his pretty boy,
    Last his sorrow, first his joy.

Weep not, my wanton, smile upon my knee ;
When thou art old there's grief enough for thee.
    Streaming tears that never stint,
    Like pearl-drops from a flint,
    Fell by course from his eyes,
    That one another's place supplies ;
    Thus he grieved in every part,
    Tears of blood fell from his heart,
    When he left his pretty boy,
    Father's sorrow, father's joy.

Weep not, my wanton, smile upon my knee ;
When thou art old there's grief enough for thee.
    The wanton smiled, father wept,
    Mother cried, baby leapt ;
    More he crowèd, more we cried,
    Nature could not sorrow hide :
    He must go, he must kiss
    Child and mother, baby bliss,

For he left his pretty boy,
Father's sorrow, father's joy.

Weep not, my wanton, smile upon my knee ;
When thou art old there's grief enough for thee.

ROBERT GREENE
*1560-1592*

*Menaphon,* 1589.

# XIII

## *Balow*

BALOW, my babe, lie still and sleep !
It grieves me sore to see thee weep.
Would'st thou be quiet I'se be glad,
Thy mourning makes my sorrow sad :
Balow, my boy, thy mother's joy,
Thy father breeds me great annoy.
           Balow, la-low !

When he began to court my love,
And with his sugar'd words me move,
His feignings false and flattering cheer
To me that time did not appear :
But now I see most cruelly
He cares neither for my babe nor me.
           Balow, la-low !

Lie still, my darling, sleep awhile,
And when thou wak'st thou'll sweetly smile :
But smile not as thy father did,
To cozen maids : nay, God forbid !
But yet I fear thou wilt go near
Thy father's heart and face to bear.
           Balow, la-low !

I cannot choose but ever will
Be loving to thy father still ;
Where'er he go, where'er he ride,
My love with him doth still abide ;
In weal or woe, where'er he go,
My heart shall ne'er depart him fro.
           Balow, la-low !

But do not, do not, pretty mine,
To feignings false thy heart incline !
Be loyal to thy lover true,
And never change her for a new :
If good or fair, of her have care
For women's banning's wondrous sare.
          Balow, la-low !

Bairn, by thy face I will beware ;
Like Sirens' words, I'll come not near ;
My babe and I together will live ;
He'll comfort me when cares do grieve.
My babe and I right soft will lie,
And ne'er respect man's cruelty.
          Balow, la-low !

Farewell, farewell, the falsest youth
That ever kissed a woman's mouth !
I wish all maids be warn'd by me
Never to trust man's courtesy ;
For if we do but chance to bow,
They'll use us then they care not how.
          Balow, la-low !

ANONYMOUS

XVIth Century. *Bishop Percy's Folio Manuscript (ed. Hales and Furnivall,* 1868).

# XIV

### *Come, Little Babe, come, Silly Soul*

COME, little babe, come, silly soul,
Thy father's shame, thy mother's grief,
Born as I doubt to all our dole,
And to thyself unhappy chief :
    Sing lullaby, and lap it warm,
    Poor soul that thinks no creature harm.

Thou little think'st and less dost know
The cause of this thy mother's moan ;
Thou want'st the wit to wail her woe,
And I myself am all alone :
    Why dost thou weep ? why dost thou wail ?
    And know'st not yet what thou dost ail.

Come, little wretch—ah, silly heart !
Mine only joy, what can I more ?
If there be any wrong thy smart,
That may the destinies implore :
    'Twas I, I say, against my will,
    I wail the time, but be thou still.

And dost thou smile ? O, thy sweet face !
Would God Himself He might thee see !—
No doubt thou would'st soon purchase grace,
I know right well, for thee and me :
    But come to mother, babe, and play,
    For father false is fled away.

Sweet boy, if it by fortune chance
Thy father home again to send,

If death do strike me with his lance,
Yet may'st thou me to him commend :
    If any ask thy mother's name,
    Tell how by love she purchased blame.

Then will his gentle heart soon yield :
I know him of a noble mind :
Although a lion in the field,
A lamb in town thou shalt him find :
    Ask blessing, babe, be not afraid,
    His sugar'd words hath me betray'd.

Then may'st thou joy and be right glad ;
Although in woe I seem to moan,
Thy father is no rascal lad,
A noble youth of blood and bone :
    His glancing looks, if he once smile,
    Right honest women may beguile.

Come, little boy, and rock asleep ;
Sing lullaby and be thou still ;
I, that can do naught else but weep,
Will sit by thee and wail my fill :
    God bless my babe, and lullaby
    From this thy father's quality.

NICHOLAS BRETON (?)
*1542-1626*

*The Arbor of Amorous Devices*, 1597.  *Stationers' Register*, 1594.

# XV

## *The Fairies' Lullaby for Titania*

You spotted snakes, with double tongue,
    Thorny hedge-hogs, be not seen ;
Newts, and blind-worms, do no wrong ;
    Come not near our fairy queen.

    Philomel, with melody,
    Sing in our sweet lullaby ;
Lulla, lulla, lullaby ; lulla, lulla, lullaby :
    Never harm, nor spell, nor charm,
    Come our lovely lady nigh :
    So, good night, with lullaby.

Weaving spiders, come not here ;
    Hence, you long-legg'd spinners, hence !
Beetles black, approach not near ;
    Worm, nor snail, do no offence.

    Philomel, with melody,
    Sing in our sweet lullaby ;
Lulla, lulla, lullaby ; lulla, lulla, lullaby :
    Never harm, nor spell, nor charm,
    Come our lovely lady nigh :
    So, good night, with lullaby.

**WILLIAM SHAKESPEARE**
*1564-1616*

*A Midsummer Night's Dream* (1600), Act II, Scene ii. Performed 1595 ?

# XVI

## *Golden Slumbers kiss your Eyes*

GOLDEN slumbers kiss your eyes,
Smiles awake you when you rise.
Sleep, pretty wantons, do not cry,
And I will sing a lullaby :
Rock them, rock them, lullaby.

Care is heavy, therefore sleep you ;
You are care, and care must keep you.
Sleep, pretty wantons, do not cry,
And I will sing a lullaby :
Rock them, rock them, lullaby.

THOMAS DEKKER
*1575-1641*

*The Pleasant Comedy of Patient Grissell* (1603) by Dekker,
Chettle and Haughton. *Stationers' Register*, 1600.

# XVII

## *Our Blessed Lady's Lullaby*

UPON my lap my sovereign sits
And sucks upon my breast ;
Meantime his love sustains my life
And gives my body rest.
     Sing lullaby, my little boy,
     Sing lullaby, mine only joy !

When thou hast taken thy repast,
Repose, my babe, on me ;
So may thy mother and thy nurse
Thy cradle also be.
     Sing lullaby, my little boy,
     Sing lullaby, mine only joy !

I grieve that duty doth not work
All that my wishing would ;
Because I would not be to thee
But in the best I should.
     Sing lullaby, my little boy,
     Sing lullaby, mine only joy !

Yet as I am, and as I may,
I must and will be thine,
Though all too little for thyself
Vouchsafing to be mine.
     Sing lullaby, my little boy,
     Sing lullaby, mine only joy !

RICHARD ROWLANDS
*alias* ROBERT VERSTEGAN
*1565-1630 ?*

*Odes*, 1601.

6, 12, 18, 24. *mine only*, emendation for *my lives.*

54

# XVIII

## *Tears*

WEEP you no more, sad fountains ;
    What need you flow so fast ?
Look how the snowy mountains
    Heaven's sun doth gently waste !
But my Sun's heavenly eyes
        View not your weeping,
        That now lies sleeping
Softly, now softly lies
        Sleeping.

Sleep is a reconciling,
    A rest that peace begets ;
Doth not the sun rise smiling
    When fair at even he sets ?
Rest you then, rest, sad eyes !
        Melt not in weeping,
        While she lies sleeping
Softly, now softly lies
        Sleeping.

**ANONYMOUS**

John Dowland's *Third and Last Book of Songs or Airs,* 1603.

# XIX

## *My Little Sweet Darling*

My little sweet darling, my comfort and joy,
      Sing lullaby, lully,
In beauty excelling the princes of Troy,
      Sing lullaby, lully.

Now suck, child, and sleep, child, thy mother's
    sweet boy !
The gods bless and keep thee from cruel annoy !
Thy father, sweet infant, from mother is gone,
And she, in the woods here, with thee left alone.

To thee, little infant, why do I make moan,
      Sing lully, lully,
Sith thou can'st not help me to sigh nor to groan,
      Sing lully, lully, lully,
      Sweet baby, lullaby,
      Sweet baby, lully, lully.

ANONYMOUS

*MS. British Musevm, Sloane* 1709.   Time of James I.

# XX

## *A Song for the Emperor Valentinian*

CARE-CHARMING Sleep, thou easer of all woes,
Brother to Death, sweetly thyself dispose
On this afflicted prince ; fall like a cloud
In gentle showers ; give nothing that is loud,
Or painful to his slumbers ; easy, light,
And as a purling stream, thou son of Night
Pass by his troubled senses, sing his pain,
Like hollow murmuring wind or silver rain ;
Into this prince gently, oh, gently slide,
And kiss him into slumbers like a bride.

JOHN FLETCHER
*1579-1625*

*Valentinian* (1647), Act v, Scene ii.   Performed 1610-1614.

# XXI

## *Sleep, Angry Beauty, Sleep*

SLEEP, angry beauty, sleep, and fear not me.
For who a sleeping lion dares provoke?
It shall suffice me here to sit and see
Those lips shut up that never kindly spoke.
    What sight can more content a lover's mind
    Than beauty seeming harmless, if not kind?

My words have charmed her, for secure she sleeps,
Though guilty much of wrong done to my love;
And, in her slumber, see! she, close-eyed, weeps:
Dreams often more than waking passions move.
    Plead, Sleep, my cause, and make her soft like
       thee,
    That she in peace may wake and pity me.

THOMAS CAMPION
*1567 ?-1619*

*The Third Book of Airs* [1617].

# XXII

## *The Virgin's Song*

SWEET was the song the Virgin sung
   When she to Bethlehem was come
And was delivered of her Son,
   That blessed Jesus hath to name.
'Sweet Babe,' quoth she, 'lull-lullaby,
   My Son and eke a Saviour born,
Who hath vouchsafèd from on high
   To visit us that were forlorn.
Lull-lullaby, Sweet Babe,' sang she,
And sweetly rocked him on her knee.

ANONYMOUS

John Attey, *The First Book of Airs*, 1622.

# XXIII

## *Song for Eumorphe*

DROP golden showers, gentle sleep ;
And all the angels of the night,
Which do us in protection keep,
Make this queen dream of delight.
Morpheus, be kind a little, and be
Death's now true image, for 'twill prove
To this poor queen that then thou art he.
Her grave is made i' th' bed of love :
Thus with sweet sweets can Heaven mix gall,
And marriage turn to funeral.

THOMAS GOFFE
*1592-1629*

*The Courageous Turk* (1632), Act II, Scene ii. Performed
1615-1623.

# XXIV

## *The Nurse's Song*

LULLABY, lullaby baby,
Great Argos' joy ;
The King of Greece thou art born to be,
In despite of Troy.
Rest ever wait upon thy head,
Sleep close thine eyes ;
The blessed guard tend on thy bed
    Of deities.
O, how this brow will beseem a crown !
How these locks will shine !
Like the rays of the sun on the ground,
These locks of thine.
The nurse of heaven still send thee milk,
May'st thou suck a queen.
Thy drink Jove's nectar, and clothes of silk,
A god may'st thou seem.
Cupid sit on this rosean cheek,
    On these ruby lips.
May thy mind like a lamb be meek
In the vales which trips.
Lullaby, lullaby baby, etc.

THOMAS GOFFE

*Orestes* (1633), Act IV, Scene i. Performed 1615-1623.

# XXV

## *Sleep, Sleep, my Soul*

SLEEP, sleep, my soul, let sorrow close thine eyes,
   Nurse fantasy records her lullabies :
Fold up thine arms, and into sighs expire,
   Deep sighs, the drowsy pages of desire.

My restless heart, whom troublous thoughts molest,
   Shall cradle thee ; thy cabin is my breast :
Where neither sun of joy, nor star of light
   Can break the mist of an affected night.

Here sadness rules ; and here thy drooping head
   Instead of down shall have a frozen bed :
Love rocks thy panting cradle : and to bring
   Thy thoughts asleep, melancholy shall sing.

And when thou wakest, to appease thy cries,
   Sad grief with tears distilling from mine eyes
Shall feed thy passion, till that bitter food
   Do surfeit it, and in my death conclude.

ANONYMOUS

*Uranus and Psyche, Bk. 2.   MS. British Museum, Addit. 40145,*
   *c.* 1630.

# XXVI

## *Calisto's Song*

Now sleep, and take thy rest,
  Once grieved and painèd wight,
Since she now loves thee best
  Who is thy heart's delight.
Let joy be thy soul's guest,
  And care be banished quite,
Since she hath thee expressed
  To be her favourite.

JAMES MABBE
*1572-1642*

*Celestina*, 1631. *Stationers' Register*, 1630.

# XXVII

## *Peace, Wayward Bairn!*

PEACE, wayward bairn ! O cease thy moan !
Thy far more wayward daddy's gone :
And never will recallèd be
By cries of either thee or me :
      For should we cry
      Until we die,
We could not scant his cruelty.
           Ballow, Ballew, etc.

He needs might in himself foresee
What thou successively might'st be ;
And could he then (though me forgo)
His infant leave, ere he did know
      How like the dad
      Would be the lad,
In time, to make fond maidens glad?
           Ballow, Ballew, etc.

RICHARD BROME
*d. 1652 ?*

*The Northern Lass* (1632), Act IV, Scene iv.

# XXVIII

## *Close Now Thine Eyes, and Rest Secure*

CLOSE now thine eyes, and rest secure ;
Thy soul is safe enough ; thy body sure ;
   He that loves thee, he that keeps
And guards thee, never slumbers, never sleeps.
The smiling conscience in a sleeping breast
   Has only peace, has only rest :
   The music and the mirth of kings
Are all but very discords, when she sings :
   Then close thine eyes and rest secure ;
No sleep so sweet as thine, no rest so sure.

FRANCIS QUARLES
*1592-1644*

*Divine Fancies*, 1632.

# XXIX

## *A Charm*

QUIET, sleep ! or I will make
Erinnys whip thee with a snake,
And cruel Rhadamanthus take
Thy body to the boiling lake,
Where fire and brimstone never slake ;
Thy heart shall burn, thy head shall ache,
And every joint about thee quake ;
And therefore dare not yet to wake !

Quiet, sleep ! or thou shalt see
The horrid hags of Tartary,
Whose tresses ugly serpents be,
And Cerberus shall bark at thee,
And all the Furies that are three—
The worst is call'd Tisiphone,—
Shall lash thee to eternity ;
And therefore sleep thou peacefully.

THOMAS RANDOLPH
*1605-1635*

*The Jealous Lovers* (1632), Act IV, Scene v.

# XXX

## Song for Leucasia

SEAL up her eyes, O sleep, but flow
Mild, as her manners, to and fro ;
Slide soft into her, that yet she
May receive no wound from thee.
And ye, present her thoughts, O dreams,
With hushing winds and purling streams.
Whiles hovering silence sits without,
Careful to keep disturbance out !
Thus seize her, sleep, thus her again resign,
So what was heaven's gift we'll reckon thine.

WILLIAM CARTWRIGHT
*1611-1643*

*The Siege : Or, Love's Convert* (1651), Act III, Scene v.   Written
c. 1637.

# XXXI

## *On a Lady Sleeping*

CALMLY as the morning's soft tears shed
Upon some rose or violet bed,
May your slumbers fall upon you,
All your thoughts sit easy on you,
Gently rocking heart and eyes
With their tuneful lullabies,
While I, till the early morrow light
Shall with your dreams have chased the night,
Like the sick flower, which, when to bed
The sun is gone, hangs the faint head
As every other warmth despising,
Will lie and wait your eyelids' fair uprising.

ANONYMOUS

*MS. British Museum Addit. 25707*, c. 1640; and *Dr. John Wilson's Autograph MS. Bodley Mus. b. 1*, before 1656.

7. *I, till*, Mr. Ault's emendation for MS. B.M. *still*, MS. Bodley *I tell*.
8. *chased*, MS. B.M. *charm'd*.

## XXXII

### *A Rocking Hymn*

SWEET baby, sleep ! What ails my dear ?
  What ails my darling thus to cry ?
Be still, my child, and lend thine ear,
  To hear me sing thy lullaby.
My pretty lamb, forbear to weep ;
Be still, my dear ; sweet baby, sleep.

Thou blessèd soul, what can'st thou fear,
  What thing to thee can mischief do ?
Thy God is now thy father dear,
  His holy Spouse thy mother too.
Sweet baby, then, forbear to weep ;
Be still, my babe ; sweet baby, sleep.

Though thy conception was in sin,
  A sacred bathing thou hast had.
And though thy birth unclean hath bin,
  A blameless babe thou now art made.
Sweet baby, then, forbear to weep ;
Be still, my dear ; sweet baby, sleep.

Whilst thus thy lullaby I sing,
  For thee great blessings ripening be ;
Thine Elder Brother is a king,
  And hath a kingdom bought for thee.
Sweet baby, then, forbear to weep ;
Be still, my babe ; sweet baby, sleep.

Sweet baby, sleep, and nothing fear ;
  For whosoever thee offends

By thy protector threatened are,
　　And God and angels are thy friends.
Sweet baby, then, forbear to weep ;
Be still, my babe ; sweet baby, sleep.

When God with us was dwelling here,
　　In little babes He took delight ;
Such innocents as thou, my dear,
　　Are ever precious in His sight.
Sweet baby, then, forbear to weep ;
Be still, my babe ; sweet baby, sleep.

A little infant once was He ;
　　And strength in weakness then was laid
Upon His Virgin-Mother's knee,
　　That power to thee might be conveyed.
Sweet baby, then, forbear to weep ;
Be still, my babe ; sweet baby, sleep.

In this thy frailty and thy need
　　He friends and helpers doth prepare,
Which thee shall cherish, clothe and feed,
　　For of thy weal they tender are.
Sweet baby, then, forbear to weep ;
Be still, my babe ; sweet baby, sleep.

The King of kings, when He was born,
　　Had not so much for outward ease ;
By Him such dressings were not worn,
　　Nor such-like swaddling-clothes as these.
Sweet baby, then, forbear to weep ;
Be still, my babe ; sweet baby, sleep.

Within a manger lodged thy Lord,
　　Where oxen lay and asses fed ;
Warm rooms we do to thee afford,
　　An easy cradle or a bed.

Sweet baby, then, forbear to weep ;
Be still, my babe ; sweet baby, sleep.

The wants that He did then sustain
   Have purchased wealth, my babe, for thee ;
And, by His torments and His pain,
   Thy rest and ease securèd be.
My baby, then, forbear to weep ;
Be still, my babe ; sweet baby, sleep.

Thou hast yet more to perfect this,
   A promise and an earnest got
Of gaining everlasting bliss,
   Though thou, my babe, perceiv'st it not.
Sweet baby, then, forbear to weep ;
Be still, my babe ; sweet baby, sleep.

GEORGE WITHER
*1588-1667*

*Haleluiah,* 1641.

# XXXIII

## *Song for Prince Mirza*

SOMNUS, the humble god that dwells
In cottages and smoky cells,
Hates gilded roofs and beds of down ;
And, though he fears no prince's frown,
Flies from the circle of a crown :

Come, I say, thou powerful god,
And thy leaden charming rod,
Dipped in the Lethean lake,
O'er his wakeful temples shake,
Lest he should sleep and never wake.

Nature, alas, why art thou so
Obligèd to thy greatest foe ?
Sleep, that is thy best repast,
Yet of death it bears a taste,
And both are the same thing at last.

SIR JOHN DENHAM
*1615-1669*

*The Sophy* (1642), Act v. Performed 1641.

# XXXIV

## *An Alarm in 1645*

BRING a light, the foe's in sight ;
    Prithee forgive me,
That I must thus leave thee in the night.
My bliss, take this, and this ;
    Sleep well, I'll keep, till
My happy return, a parting kiss.
    Thou would'st free my life from fears,
        Yet thy wet eye
    Drowns me with tears ;
    Wipe those fair pearls from thine eye,
        And hear thy soldier's
    Lullaby.

Sweet, sleep !  Lie still, my dear !
    Dangers be strangers
For ever, unto thy eye or ear ;
No sounds, or woe for wounds
    Number thy slumbers,
Or dare to approach within thy bounds ;
    But such songs as seraphs sing,
        Which move by love
    Unto their King :
    That thy sight, touch, taste, or smells
        May say, all joy
    In hearing dwells.

And when thou wakest again,
    Fortune importune
Thy senses to see us happy men :
That we may so agree,

73

Dangers of strangers
May never destroy our unity :
So shall peace ascend her throne,
For than each man
May claim his own.
We like raging seas will run,
That meet and fight,
Then flow in one.

THOMAS JORDAN
*1612 ?-1685*

*Divinity and Morality in Robes of Poetry* [no date].

32. *than*, then.

# XXXV

*She Sleeps.   Peace Crown Thine Eyes!*

SHE sleeps.   Peace crown thine eyes !   Sweet
    dreams in deep,
Softest security thy senses steep !
Aye me ! she groans.   Sadly, alas, oppressed
Lies the dear bosom gasping without rest.
Sickness, not sleep's numb hand, her eyes' faint ray
And those dead ashes of her cheek bewray,
Whose ominous hue (as bent t' invert our years)
Like winter's snow on April buds appears.
So the vexed morn from her sere lover's bed
And cold embraces, with a look of lead,
Pale and delightless rises ; the autumn bower
So wanes, so falling droops the evening flower,
As life this fair declining lamp of light
(Her shine contracting) all o'erhaled in night.

ANONYMOUS

*Dr. John Wilson's Autograph MS. Bodley Mus. b. 1, before 1656.*

# XXXVI

## *Song*

SET BY MR. COLEMAN

SEE how like twilight slumber falls
T' obscure the glory of those balls,
    And, as she sleeps,
    See how light creeps
Thorough the chinks, and beautifies
The rayey fringe of her fair eyes.

Observe love's feuds, how fast they fly
To every heart from her closed eye ;
    What then will she,
    When waking, be ?
A glowing light for all t' admire,
Such as would set the world on fire.

Then seal her eyelids, gentle sleep,
Whiles cares of her mine open keep ;
    Lock up, I say,
    Those doors of day,
Which with the morn for lustre strive,
That I may look on her, and live.

CHARLES COTTON
*1630-1687*

*Poems on Several Occasions*, 1689.  Written 1650-1660 ?

# XXXVII

## *Laura Weeping*

### ODE

WINDS, whisper gently whilst she sleeps,
    And fan her with your cooling wings ;
Whilst she her drops of beauty weeps
    From pure and yet-unrivalled springs.

Glide over beauty's field, her face,
    To kiss her lip and cheek be bold,
But with a calm and stealing pace,
    Neither too rude, nor yet too cold.

Play in her beams and crisp her hair
    With such a gale as wings soft love,
And with so sweet, so rich an air,
    As breathes from the Arabian grove.

A breath as hushed as lover's sigh,
    Or that unfolds the morning door ;
Sweet as the winds that gently fly
    To sweep the spring's enamelled floor.

Murmur soft music to her dreams,
    That pure and unpolluted run,
Like to the new-born crystal streams
    Under the bright enamoured sun.

But when she waking shall display
    Her light, retire within your bar ;
Her breath is life, her eyes are day,
    And all mankind her creatures are.

CHARLES COTTON

*Ibid.*

# XXXVIII

## *On a Child Sleeping in Cynthia's Lap*

SLEEP, happy boy, there sleep and take thy rest,
Free from the passions which disturb my breast ;
Yet know 'tis Innocence that thee has freed
And lets thee sleep so quiet on this bed.

Thy wearied limbs have sweetly rested here,
If with less sun, in a more happy sphere ;
Whilst in despair my soul afflicted lies,
And of mere envy to behold thee, dies.

Dream thou enjoy'st more true felicity
Than lavish fortune can bestow on thee ;
That thou amidst such precious gems art hurl'd
Are able to enrich th' insatiate world :

That thou the Phoenix shalt transcend in fame,
Who sleep'st and risest in a purer flame ;
That thou'rt an Angel, Heav'n's that lap I view :
Yet all this while it is no dream, but true.

PHILIP AYRES
*1638-1712*

*Lyric Poems*, 1687.

# XXXIX

## *A Cradle Hymn*

Hush ! my dear, lie still and slumber ;
  Holy angels guard thy bed !
Heavenly blessings without number
  Gently falling on thy head.

Sleep, my babe ; thy food and raiment,
  House and home, thy friends provide ;
All without thy care or payment,
  All thy wants are well supplied.

How much better thou'rt attended
  Than the Son of God could be,
When from heaven He descended
  And became a child like thee !

Soft and easy is thy cradle :
  Coarse and hard thy Saviour lay,
When His birthplace was a stable
  And His softest bed was hay.

Blessèd babe ! what glorious features—
  Spotless fair, divinely bright !
Must He dwell with brutal creatures ?
  How could angels bear the sight ?

Was there nothing but a manger
  Cursèd sinners could afford
To receive the heavenly stranger ?
  Did they thus affront their Lord ?

Soft, my child : I did not chide thee,
  Though my song might sound too hard ;
'Tis thy { *Mother
          Nurse that } sits beside thee,
  And her arm shall be thy guard.

Yet to read the shameful story
  How the Jews abused their King,
How they served the Lord of Glory,
  Makes me angry while I sing.

See the kinder shepherds round Him,
  Telling wonders from the sky !
Where they sought Him, there they found Him,
  With His Virgin-Mother by.

See the lovely babe a-dressing ;
  Lovely infant, how He smiled !
When He wept, the mother's blessing
  Soothed and hushed the holy child.

Lo, He slumbers in His manger,
  Where the hornèd oxen fed :
Peace, my darling, here's no danger,
  Here's no ox anear thy bed.

'Twas to save thee, child, from dying,
  Save my dear from burning flame,
Bitter groans and endless crying,
  That thy blest Redeemer came.

May'st thou live to know and fear Him,
  Trust and love Him all thy days !
Then go dwell for ever near Him,
  See His face, and sing His praise !

* Here you may use the words, *Brother, Sister, Neighbour, Friend*, etc.

I could give thee thousand kisses,
   Hoping what I most desire :
Not a mother's fondest wishes
   Can to greater joys aspire.

ISAAC WATTS
*1674-1748*

*Divine Songs,* 1720.

# XL

## A Song

*Imitated from ' The Midsummer Night's Dream ' of
Shakespeare, Act ii, Scene v.*

Lo here, beneath this hallow'd shade
  Within a cowslip's blossom deep,
The lovely queen of Elves is laid ;
  May nought disturb her balmy sleep !

Let not the snake or baleful toad
  Approach the silent mansion near,
Or newt profane the sweet abode,
  Or owl repeat her orgies here.

No snail or worm shall hither come
  With noxious filth her bow'r to stain :
Hence be the beetle's sullen hum,
  And spider's disembowel'd train.

The love-lorn nightingale alone
  Shall thro' Zitania's arbour stray,
To sooth her sleep with melting moan,
  And lull her with his sweetest lay.

THOMAS WARTON THE YOUNGER
*1728-1790*

Robert Dodsley's *Museum*, 1746.

# XLI

## *Ode*

O GENTLE, feather-footed Sleep,
In downy dews her temples steep,
Softly waving o'er her head
Thy care-beguiling rod of lead ;
Let Hymen in her dreams appear
And mildly whisper in her ear,
That constant hearts can never prove
True transports, but in wedded love.

JOSEPH WARTON
*1722-1800*

Chalmers' *English Poets*, 1810.   Written *c.* 1747 ?

# XLII

## *A Cradle Song*

SWEET dreams, form a shade
O'er my lovely infant's head ;
Sweet dreams of pleasant streams
By happy, silent, moony beams.

Sweet sleep, with soft down
Weave thy brows an infant crown.
Sweet sleep, Angel mild,
Hover o'er my happy child.

Sweet smiles, in the night
Hover over my delight ;
Sweet smiles, Mother's smiles,
All the livelong night beguiles.

Sweet moans, dovelike sighs,
Chase not slumber from thy eyes.
Sweet moans, sweeter smiles,
All the dovelike moans beguiles.

Sleep, sleep, happy child,
All creation slept and smil'd ;
Sleep, sleep, happy sleep,
While o'er thee thy mother weep.

Sweet babe, in thy face
Holy image I can trace.
Sweet babe, once like thee,
Thy Maker lay and wept for me,

Wept for me, for thee, for all,
When He was an infant small.
Thou His image ever see,
Heavenly face that smiles on thee,

Smiles on thee, on me, on all ;
Who became an infant small.
Infant smiles are His own smiles ;
Heaven and earth to peace beguiles.

WILLIAM BLAKE
*1757-1827*

*Songs of Innocence*, 1789.

# XLIII

## *A Cradle Song*

SLEEP ! sleep ! beauty bright,
Dreaming o'er the joys of night ;
Sleep ! sleep ! in thy sleep
Little sorrows sit and weep.

Sweet Babe, in thy face
Soft desires I can trace,
Secret joys and secret smiles,
Little pretty infant wiles.

As thy softest limbs I feel,
Smiles as of the morning steal
O'er thy cheek, and o'er thy breast
Where thy little heart does rest.

O ! the cunning wiles that creep
In thy little heart asleep.
When thy little heart does wake
Then the dreadful lightnings break,

From thy cheek and from thy eye,
O'er the youthful harvests nigh.
Infant wiles and infant smiles
Heaven and Earth of peace beguiles.

WILLIAM BLAKE

*Rossetti MS.*, 1793.

# XLIV

## *The Highland Balou*

HEE balou, my sweet wee Donald,
Picture o' the great Clanronald !
Brawlie kens our wanton Chief
Wha gat my young Highland thief.

Leeze me on thy bonie craigie !
An thou live, thou'll steal a naigie,
Travel the country thro' and thro',
And bring hame a Carlisle cow !

Thro' the Lawlands, o'er the Border,
Weel, my babie, may thou furder !
Herry the louns o' the laigh Countrie,
Syne to the Highlands hame to me !

ROBERT BURNS
*1759-1796*

James Johnson, *The Scots Musical Museum*, Vol. V. No. 472.
1796.

1. *balou*, lullaby.
5. *Leeze me on*, blessings on ; *bonie craigie*, pretty throat.
6. *naigie*, nag.                    10. *furder*, succeed.
11. *Herry the louns*, Harry the rogues ; *laigh*, low.
12. *Syne*, Then.

# XLV

## *Cradle Song*

BALOO, baloo, my wee wee thing,
  O saftly close thy blinkin' e'e !
Baloo, baloo, my wee wee thing,
  For thou art doubly dear to me.
Thy daddy now is far awa',
  A sailor laddie o'er the sea ;
But hope aye hechts his safe return
  To you, my bonnie lamb, and me.

Baloo, baloo, my wee wee thing,
  O saftly close thy blinkin' e'e !
Baloo, baloo, my wee wee thing,
  For thou art doubly dear to me.
Thy face is simple, sweet, and mild,
  Like ony simmer e'ening fa' ;
Thy sparkling e'e is bonnie black ;
  Thy neck is like the mountain snaw.

Baloo, baloo, my wee wee thing,
  O saftly close thy blinkin' e'e !
Baloo, baloo, my wee wee thing,
  For thou art doubly dear to me.
O, but thy daddie's absence, lang,
  Might break my dowie heart in twa,
Wert thou na left, a dawtit pledge,
  To steal the eerie hours awa.

RICHARD GALL
*1776-1801*

*Poems and Songs*, 1819.

7. *hechts*, promises.          22. *dowie*, dejected.
23. *dawtit*, unpretentious.

# XLVI

## The Lullaby of a Female Convict to her Child the Night Previous to Execution

SLEEP, baby mine, enkerchieft on my bosom,
    Thy cries they pierce again my bleeding breast ;
Sleep, baby mine, not long thou'lt have a mother
    To lull thee fondly in her arms to rest.

Baby, why dost thou keep this sad complaining ?
    Long from mine eyes have kindly slumbers fled ;
Hush, hush, my babe, the night is quickly waning,
    And I would fain compose my aching head.

Poor wayward wretch ! and who will heed thy
    weeping,
    When soon an outcast on the world thou'lt be ?
Who then will soothe thee, when thy mother's
    sleeping
    In her low grave of shame and infamy ?

Sleep, baby mine—To-morrow I must leave thee,
    And I would snatch an interval of rest :
Sleep these last moments, ere the laws bereave thee,
    For never more thou'lt press a mother's breast.

HENRY KIRKE WHITE
*1785-1806*

*Remains*, 1808.

# XLVII

## *The Virgin's Cradle Hymn*

*Copied from a print of the Virgin in a Roman Catholic village in Germany*

DORMI, Jesu ! Mater ridet
Quae tam dulcem somnum videt,
    Dormi, Jesu ! blandule !
Si non dormis, Mater plorat
Inter fila cantans orat,
    Blande, veni, somnule.


### ENGLISH

SLEEP, sweet babe ! my cares beguiling :
Mother sits beside thee smiling ;
    Sleep, my darling, tenderly !
If thou sleep not, mother mourneth,
Singing as her wheel she turneth :
    Come, soft slumber, balmily.

SAMUEL TAYLOR COLERIDGE
*1772-1834*

*The Courier*, August 30, 1811.

# XLVIII

## *The Spectre's Cradle Song*

Hush, my bonny babe ! hush, and be still !
Thy mother's arms shall shield thee from ill.
Far have I borne thee, in sorrow and pain,
To drink the breeze of the world again.
The dew shall moisten thy brow so meek,
And the breeze of midnight fan thy cheek,
And soon shall we rest in the bow of the hill ;
Hush, my bonny babe ! hush, and be still !
For thee have I travelled, in weakness and woe,
The world above and the world below.
My heart was soft, and it fell in the snare :
Thy father was cruel, but thou wert fair.
I sinned, I sorrowed, I died for thee ;
Smile, my bonny babe ! smile on me !

See yon thick clouds of murky hue ;
Yon star that peeps from its window blue ;
Above yon clouds, that wander far,
Away, above yon little star,
There's a home of peace that shall soon be thine,
And there shalt thou see thy Father and mine.
The flowers of the world shall bud and decay,
The trees of the forest be weeded away ;
But there shalt *thou* bloom for ever and aye.
The time will come, I shall follow thee ;
But long, long hence that time shall be ;
O weep not thou for thy mother's ill ;
Hush, my bonny babe ! hush, and be still !

JAMES HOGG
*1770-1835*

*The Queen's Wake*, 1813.  (Dedicated. 1811.)

# XLIX

## *On a Girl Asleep*

SLEEP on, and dream of Heav'n awhile.
Though shut so close thy laughing eyes,
Thy rosy lips still seem to smile,
And move, and breathe delicious sighs !—

Ah, now soft blushes tinge her cheeks,
And mantle o'er her neck of snow.
Ah, now she murmurs, now she speaks
What most I wish—and fear to know.

She starts, she trembles, and she weeps !
Her fair hands folded on her breast.
—And now, how like a saint she sleeps !
A seraph in the realms of rest !

Sleep on secure !  Above control,
Thy thoughts belong to Heav'n and thee !
And may the secret of thy soul
Repose within its sanctuary !

SAMUEL ROGERS
*1763-1855*

*Poems,* 1812.

# L

## *Asleep*

ASLEEP ! O sleep a little while, white pearl !
And let me kneel, and let me pray to thee,
And let me call Heaven's blessing on thine eyes,
And let me breathe into the happy air,
That doth enfold and touch thee all about,
Vows of my slavery, my giving up,
My sudden adoration, my great love !

JOHN KEATS
*1795-1821*

R. M. Milnes' *Life, Letters, and Literary Remains of John Keats,*
 1848. Written 1818.

# LI

## *Lullaby of an Infant Chief*

Air—' Cadil gu lo.'

O HUSH thee, my babie, thy sire was a knight ;
Thy mother a lady, both lovely and bright ;
The woods and the glens, from the towers which we
    see,
They all are belonging, dear baby, to thee.
        O ho ro, i ri ri, cadil gu lo,
        O ho ro, i ri ri, cadil gu lo.

O fear not the bugle, though loudly it blows,
It calls but the warders that guard thy repose ;
Their bows would be bended, their blades would be
    red,
Ere the step of a foeman draws near to thy bed.
        O ho ro, i ri ri, cadil gu lo,
        O ho ro, i ri ri, cadil gu lo.

O hush thee, my baby, the time soon will come,
When thy sleep shall be broken by trumpet and
    drum ;
Then hush thee, my darling, take rest while you
    may,
For strife comes with manhood, and waking with
    day.
        O ho ro, i ri ri, cadil gu lo,
        O ho ro, i ri ri, cadil gu lo.

SIR WALTER SCOTT
*1771-1832*

*Poetical Works,* 1820.

    5. *cadil gu lo,* sleep on till day.

# LII

## *Maudra's Song over her Infant Boy*

O SLEEP, my babe, hear not the rippling wave,
Nor feel the breeze that round thee lingering strays,
  To drink thy balmy breath,
  And sigh one long farewell.

Soon shall it mourn above thy wat'ry bed,
And whisper to me, on the wave-beat shore,
  Deep murm'ring in reproach,
  Thy sad untimely fate.

Ere those dear eyes had open'd on the light,
In vain to plead, thy coming life was sold,
  O ! wakened but to sleep,
  Whence it can wake no more !

A thousand and a thousand silken leaves
The tufted beech unfolds in early spring,
  All clad in tenderest green,
  All of the self-same shape :

A thousand infant faces, soft and sweet,
Each year sends forth, yet every mother views
  Her last not least beloved
  Like its dear self alone.

No musing mind hath ever yet foreshaped
The face to-morrow's sun shall first reveal,
  No heart hath e'er conceived
  · What love that face will bring.

95

O sleep, my babe, nor heed how mourns the gale
To part with thy soft locks and fragrant breath,
    As when it deeply sighs
    O'er autumn's latest bloom.

SARA COLERIDGE
*1802-1850*

*Phantasmion*, 1837.

# LIII

## *The Virgin Mary to the Child Jesus*

But see the Virgin blest
Hath laid her babe to rest.
                    MILTON's *Hymn on the Nativity.*

### I

SLEEP, sleep, mine Holy One !
My flesh, my Lord !—what name ?   I do not know
A name that seemeth not too high or low,
        Too far from me or heaven.
My Jesus, *that* is best ! that word being given
By the majestic angel whose command
Was softly as a man's beseeching said,
When I and all the earth appeared to stand
        In the great overflow
Of light celestial from his wings and head.
        Sleep, sleep, my saving One !

### II

And art Thou come for saving, baby-browed
And speechless Being—art Thou come for saving ?
The palm that grows beside our door is bowed
By treadings of the low wind from the south,
A restless shadow through the chamber waving :
Upon its bough a bird sings in the sun ;
But Thou, with that close slumber on Thy mouth,
Dost seem of wind and sun already weary.
Art come for saving, O my weary One !

### III

Perchance this sleep that shutteth out the dreary
Earth-sounds and motions, opens on Thy soul

High dreams on fire with God ;
High songs that make the pathways where they
    roll
More bright than stars do theirs ; and visions new
Of Thine eternal Nature's old abode.
      Suffer this mother's kiss,
      Best thing that earthly is,
To glide the music and the glory through,
Nor narrow in Thy dream the broad upliftings
      Of any seraph wing.
Thus noiseless, thus. Sleep, sleep, my dreaming
    One !

### IV

The slumber of His lips meseems to run
Through *my* lips to mine heart,—to all its shiftings
Of sensual life, bringing contrariousness
In a great calm. I feel I could lie down
As Moses did, and die,*—and then live most.
I am 'ware of you, heavenly Presences,
That stand with your peculiar light unlost,
Each forehead with a high thought for a crown,
Unsunned i' the sunshine ! I am 'ware. Ye
    throw
No shade against the wall ! How motionless
Ye round me with your living statuary,
While through your whiteness, in and outwardly,
Continual thoughts of God appear to go,
Like light's soul in itself. I bear, I bear,
To look upon the dropt lids of your eyes,
Though their external shining testifies
To that beatitude within, which were
Enough to blast an eagle at his sun.
I fall not on my sad clay face before ye,—
      I look on His. I know

* ' It is a Jewish tradition that Moses died of the kisses of God's lips.'

My spirit which dilateth with the woe
    Of His mortality
    May well contain your glory.
    Yea, drop your lids more low.
Ye are but fellow-worshippers with me !
    Sleep, sleep, my worshipped One !

### V

We sate among the stalls at Bethlehem.
The dumb kine from their fodder turning them,
    Softened their hornèd faces
    To almost human gazes
    Toward the newly Born :
The simple shepherds from the star-lit brooks
    Brought visionary looks,
As yet in their astonied hearing rung
    The strange, sweet angel-tongue :
The magi of the East, in sandals worn,
    Knelt reverent, sweeping round,
With long pale beards, their gifts upon the ground,
    The incense, myrrh, and gold
These baby hands were impotent to hold.
So, let all earthlies and celestials wait
    Upon Thy royal state.
    Sleep, sleep, my kingly One !

### VI

I am not proud—meek angels, ye invest
New meeknesses to hear such utterance rest
On mortal lips,—' I am not proud '—*not proud* !
Albeit in my flesh God sent His Son,
Albeit over Him my head is bowed
As others bow before Him, still mine heart
Bows lower than their knees.   O centuries
That roll, in vision, your futurities
   ·My future grave athwart,—

Whose murmurs seem to reach me while I keep
          Watch o'er this sleep,—
Say of me as the Heavenly said—' Thou art
The blessedest of women ! '—blessedest,
Not holiest, not noblest—no high name,
Whose height misplaced may pierce me like
    a shame,
When I sit meek in heaven !
                              For me, for me,
God knows that I am feeble like the rest !—
I often wandered forth, more child than maiden,
Among the midnight hills of Galilee
          Whose summits looked heaven-laden,
Listening to silence as it seemed to be
God's voice, so soft yet strong—so fain to
    press
Upon my heart as heaven did on the height,
And waken up its shadows by a light,
And show its vileness by a holiness.
Then I knelt down most silent like the night,
          Too self-renounced for fears,
Raising my small face to the boundless blue
Whose stars did mix and tremble in my tears :
God heard *them* falling after—with His dew.


                         VII

So, seeing my corruption, can I see
This Incorruptible now born of me,
This fair new Innocence no sun did chance
To shine on (for even Adam was no child),
Created from my nature all defiled,
This mystery, from out mine ignorance,—
Nor feel the blindness, stain, corruption, more
Than others do, or *I* did heretofore ?—
Can hands wherein such burden pure has been,
Not open with the cry ' unclean, unclean,'

More oft than any else beneath the skies ?
     Ah King, ah Christ, ah son !
The kine, the shepherds, the abasèd wise,
     Must all less lowly wait
     Than I, upon thy state.—
     Sleep, sleep, my kingly One !

### VIII

Art Thou a King, then ?   Come, His universe,
     Come, crown me Him a King !
Pluck rays from all such stars as never fling
     Their light where fell a curse,
And make a crowning for this kingly brow !—
What is my word ?—Each empyreal star
     Sits in a sphere afar
     In shining ambuscade.
     The child-brow, crowned by none,
     Keeps its unchildlike shade.
     Sleep, sleep, my crownless One !

### IX

Unchildlike shade !—No other babe doth wear
An aspect very sorrowful, as Thou.—
No small babe-smiles, my watching heart has seen,
To float like speech the speechless lips between :
No dovelike cooing in the golden air,
No quick short joys of leaping babyhood.
     Alas, our earthly good
In heaven thought evil, seems too good for Thee :
     Yet, sleep, my weary One !

### X

And then the drear sharp tongue of prophecy,
With the dread sense of things which shall be done,
Doth smite me inly, like a sword ! a sword ?—

(*That* 'smites the Shepherd.') Then, I think
    aloud
The words ' despised,'—' rejected,'—every word
Recoiling into darkness as I view
    The DARLING on my knee.
Bright angels,—move not !—lest ye stir the cloud
Betwixt my soul and His futurity !
I must not die, with mother's work to do,
    And could not live—and see.

## XI

It is enough to bear
This image still and fair—
This holier in sleep,
Than a saint at prayer ;
This aspect of a child
Who never sinned or smiled ;
This Presence in an infant's face,
This sadness most like love,
This love than love more deep,
This weakness like omnipotence
It is so strong to move.
Awful is this watching place,
Awful what I see from hence—
A king, without regalia,
A God, without the thunder,
A child, without the heart for play ;
Aye, a Creator, rent asunder
From His first glory and cast away
On His own world, for me alone
To hold in hands created, crying—SON !

## XII

That tear fell not on Thee,
Beloved, yet Thou stirrest in Thy slumber !
THOU, stirring not for glad sounds out of number

Which through the vibratory palm-trees run
　　From summer wind and bird,
　　So quickly hast Thou heard
　　A tear fall silently ?
　　Wak'st Thou, O loving One ?

ELIZABETH BARRETT BROWNING
*1806-1861*

*The Seraphim, and Other Poems,* 1838.

# LIV

## *The Last Cradle Song*

AIR—' My Love's shoulders are broad and square '

*A Border Melody*

BAWLOO, my bonnie baby, bawlillilu,
  Light be thy care and cumber ;
Bawloo, my bonnie baby, bawlillilu,
  O sweet be thy sinless slumber.
Ere thou wert born my youthful heart
  Yearned o'er my babe with sorrow ;
Long is the night-noon that we must part,
  But bright shall arise the morrow.

Bawloo, my bonnie baby, bawlillilu,
  Here no more will I see thee ;
Bawloo, my bonnie baby, bawlillilu,
  O sair is my heart to lea' thee.
But far within yon sky so blue,
  In love that fail shall never,
In valleys beyond the land of the dew,
  I'll sing to my baby for ever.

JAMES HOGG
*1770-1835*

*The Poetical Works of the Ettrick Shepherd,* 1840.

2. *cumber*, trouble, distress.

# LV

## *Sleep, Ellen Aubrey, Sleep*

SLEEP, Ellen Aubrey, sleep, and dream of me :
Sleep, Ellen, folded in thy sister's arm,
And sleeping, haply dream her arm is mine.

Sleep, Ellen, folded in Emilia's arm ;
Emilia, fairer than all else but thou,
For thou art fairer than all else that is.

Sleep, breathing health and peace upon her breast :
Sleep, breathing love and trust against her lip :
I go to-night : I come to-morrow morn.

I go, but I return : I would I were
The pilot of the darkness and the dream.
Sleep, Ellen Aubrey, love, and dream of me.

ALFRED, LORD TENNYSON
*1809-1892*

From *Audley Court*, in *Poems*, 1842.

# LVI

## Sleeping and Watching

### I

SLEEP on, baby, on the floor,
　Tired of all the playing !
Sleep with smile the sweeter for
　That, you dropped away in !
On your curls' full roundness, stand
　Golden lights serenely ;
One cheek, pushed out by the hand,
　Folds the dimple inly.
Little head and little foot
　Heavy laid for pleasure,
Underneath the lids half shut,
　Slants the shining azure.—
Open-soul in noonday sun,
　So, you lie and slumber !
Nothing evil having done,
　Nothing can encumber.

### II

I, who cannot sleep as well,
　Shall I sigh to view you ?
Or sigh further to foretell
　All that may undo you ?
Nay, keep smiling, little child,
　Ere the sorrow neareth :
I will smile too ! patience mild
　Pleasure's token weareth.
Nay, keep sleeping before loss :
　I shall sleep though losing !

As by cradle, so by cross,
  Sure is the reposing.

### III

And God knows who sees us twain,
  Child at childish leisure,
I am near as tired of pain
  As you seem of pleasure.
Very soon too, by His grace
  Gently wrapt around me,
Shall I show as calm a face,
  Shall I sleep as soundly.
Differing in this, that you
  Clasp your playthings, sleeping,
While my hand shall drop the few
  Given to my keeping :
Differing in this, that I
  Sleeping shall be colder,
And in waking presently,
  Brighter to beholder :
Differing in this beside
  (Sleeper, have you heard me ?
Do you move, and open wide
  Eyes of wonder toward me ?)—
That while you, I thus recall
  From your sleep, I solely,
Me from mine an angel shall,
  With reveillie holy.

E. B. BROWNING

*Graham's Magazine*, September, 1843.

# LVII

## *The Child Asleep*

### *(From the French)*

SWEET babe ! true portrait of thy father's face,
 Sleep on the bosom that thy lips have pressed !
Sleep, little one ; and closely, gently place
 Thy drowsy eyelid on thy mother's breast.

Upon that tender eye, my little friend,
 Soft sleep shall come, that cometh not to me !
I watch to see thee, nourish thee, defend ;—
 'Tis sweet to watch for thee,—alone for thee !

His arms fall down ; sleep sits upon his brow ;
 His eye is closed ; he sleeps, nor dreams of harm.
Wore not his cheek the apple's ruddy glow,
 Would you not say he slept on Death's cold arm ?

Awake, my boy !—I tremble with affright !
 Awake, and chase this fatal thought !—Unclose
Thine eye but for one moment on the light !
 Even at the price of thine, give me repose !

Sweet error !—he but slept,—I breathe again ;—
 Come, gentle dreams, the hour of sleep beguile !
O ! when shall he, for whom I sigh in vain,
 Beside me watch to see thy waking smile ?

HENRY WADSWORTH LONGFELLOW
*1807-1882*

*Poems,* 1845.

# LVIII

### *Sweet and Low*

SWEET and low, sweet and low,
  Wind of the western sea,
Low, low, breathe and blow,
  Wind of the western sea !
Over the rolling waters go,
Come from the dying moon, and blow,
  Blow him again to me ;
While my little one, while my pretty one, sleeps.

Sleep and rest, sleep and rest,
  Father will come to thee soon ;
Rest, rest, on mother's breast,
  Father will come to thee soon ;
Father will come to his babe in the nest,
Silver sails all out of the west
  Under the silver moon :
Sleep, my little one, sleep, my pretty one, sleep.

TENNYSON

*The Princess*, 1850.

# LIX

## *What Does Little Birdie Say?*

WHAT does little birdie say
In her nest at peep of day?
Let me fly, says little birdie,
Mother, let me fly away.
Birdie, rest a little longer,
Till the little wings are stronger.
So she rests a little longer,
Then she flies away.

What does little baby say,
In her bed at peep of day?
Baby says, like little birdie,
Let me rise and fly away.
Baby, sleep a little longer,
Till the little limbs are stronger.
If she sleeps a little longer,
Baby too shall fly away.

TENNYSON

From *Sea Dreams*, in *Macmillan's Magazine*, January, 1860.

# LX

## *To a Sleeping Child*

Lips, lips, open !
Up comes a little bird that lives inside,
Up comes a little bird, and peeps and out he flies.

All the day he sits inside, and sometimes he sings,
Up he comes and out he goes at night to spread his
    wings.

Little bird, little bird, whither will you go ?
Round about the world while nobody can know.

Little bird, little bird, whither do you flee ?
Far away round the world while nobody can see.

Little bird, little bird, how long will you roam ?
All round the world and around again home ;

Round the round world, and back through the air,
When the morning comes, the little bird is there.

Back comes the little bird, and looks, and in he flies.
Up wakes the little boy, and opens both his eyes.

Sleep, sleep, little boy, little bird's away,
Little bird will come again, by the peep of day ;

Sleep, sleep, little boy, little bird must go
Round about the world, while nobody can know.

Sleep, sleep sound, little bird goes round,
Round and round he goes—sleep, sleep sound.

ARTHUR HUGH CLOUGH
*1819-1861*

*Poems*, 1862.

# LXI

## *Lullaby, Oh, Lullaby!*

LULLABY, oh, lullaby !
Flowers are closed and lambs are sleeping ;
   Lullaby, oh, lullaby !
Stars are up, the moon is peeping ;
   Lullaby, oh, lullaby !
While the birds are silence keeping,
   (Lullaby, oh, lullaby !)
Sleep, my baby, fall a-sleeping,
   Lullaby, oh, lullaby !

CHRISTINA GEORGINA ROSSETTI
*1830-1894*

*Sing-Song*, 1872.

# LXII

## *Lullaby*

THE rook's nest do rock on the tree-top
Where vew foes can stand ;
The martin's is high, an' is deep
In the steep cliff o' zand.
But thou, love, a-sleepèn where vootsteps
Mid come to thy bed,
Hast father an' mother to watch thee
An' shelter thy head.
　　　　Lullaby, Lilybrow.　Lie asleep ;
　　　　Blest be thy rest.

An' zome birds do keep under ruffèn
Their young vrom the storm,
An' zome wi' nest hoodèns o' moss
An' o' wool, do lie warm.
An' we wull look well to the house-ruf
That o'er thee mid leäk,
An' the blast that mid beät on thy winder
Shall not smite thy cheäk.
　　　　Lullaby, Lilibrow.　Lie asleep ;
　　　　Blest be thy rest.

WILLIAM BARNES
1801-1886

*Poems of Rural Life in the Dorset Dialect*, 1879.

## LXIII

*Cradle Songs*

(*To a tune of Blake's*)

### I

Baby, baby bright,
Sleep can steal from sight
Little of your light :

Soft as fire in dew,
Still the life in you
Lights your slumber through.

Four white eyelids keep
Fast the seal of sleep
Deep as love is deep :

Yet, though closed it lies,
Love behind them spies
Heaven in two blue eyes.

### II

Baby, baby dear,
Earth and heaven are near
Now, for heaven is here.

Heaven is every place
Where your flower-sweet face
Fills our eyes with grace.

Till your own eyes deign
Earth a glance again,
Earth and heaven are twain.

114

Now your sleep is done,
Shine, and show the sun
Earth and heaven are one.

### III

Baby, baby sweet,
Love's own lips are meet
Scarce to kiss your feet.

Hardly love's own ear,
When your laugh crows clear,
Quite deserves to hear.

Hardly love's own wile,
Though it please awhile,
Quite deserves your smile.

Baby full of grace,
Bless us yet a space :
Sleep will come apace.

### IV

Baby, baby true,
Man, whate'er he do,
May deceive not you.

Smiles whose love is guile,
Worn a flattering while,
Win from you no smile.

One, the smile alone
Out of love's heart grown,
Ever wins your own.

Man, a dunce uncouth,
Errs in age and youth :
Babies know the truth.

Baby, baby fair,
Love is fain to dare
Bless your haughtiest air.

Baby blithe and bland,
Reach but forth a hand
None may dare withstand ;

Love, though wellnigh cowed,
Yet would praise aloud
Pride so sweetly proud.

No ! the fitting word
Even from breeze or bird
Never yet was heard.

Baby, baby kind,
Though no word we find,
Bear us yet in mind.

Half a little hour,
Baby bright in bower,
Keep this thought aflower—

Love it is, I see,
Here with heart and knee
Bows and worships me.

What can baby do,
Then, for love so true ?—
Let it worship you.

Baby, baby wise,
Love's divine surmise
Lights your constant eyes.

Day and night and day
One mute word would they,
As the soul saith, say.

Trouble comes and goes ;
Wonder ebbs and flows ;
Love remains and glows.

As the fledgeling dove
Feels the breast above,
So your heart feels love.

ALGERNON CHARLES SWINBURNE
*1837-1909*

*A Midsummer Holiday and Other Poems*, 1884.

# LXIV

## *A Christmas Lullaby*

Sleep, baby, sleep ! The Mother sings :
Heaven's angels kneel and fold their wings :
　　Sleep, baby, sleep !

With swathes of scented hay thy bed
By Mary's hand at eve was spread.
　　Sleep, baby, sleep !

At midnight came the shepherds, they
Whom seraphs wakened by the way.
　　Sleep, baby, sleep !

And three kings from the East afar
Ere dawn came guided by thy star.
　　Sleep, baby, sleep !

They brought thee gifts of gold and gems,
Pure orient pearls, rich diadems.
　　Sleep, baby, sleep !

But thou who liest slumbering there,
Art King of kings, earth, ocean, air.
　　Sleep, baby, sleep !

Sleep, baby, sleep ! The shepherds sing :
Through heaven, through earth, hosannas ring.
　　Sleep, baby, sleep !

JOHN ADDINGTON SYMONDS
*1840-1893*

A. H. Bullen, *A Christmas Garland,* 1885.

## LXV

### *A Cradle Song*

THE angels are stooping
Above your bed ;
They weary of trooping
With the whimpering dead.

God's laughing in heaven
To see you so good ;
The shining Seven
Are gay with His mood.

I kiss you and kiss you,
My pigeon, my own ;
Ah, how I shall miss you
When you have grown !

WILLIAM BUTLER YEATS
b. *1865*

*The Scots Observer*, April 19, 1890.

# NOTES

The original spelling has been preserved in poems earlier than 1500, except that *I* is substituted for the personal pronoun *i* or *y*, *is* for *ys*, *v* for consonantal *u*, *and* for *&*, *th* for *þ*, and *y*, *gh*, and once *h* (*deth*, II, 36) for ȝ. The long line of the MSS. has been subdivided into two short lines in I, II, and IV. In IV and V the refrain (italicised) is, as in the MSS., placed at the beginning of the poem only ; elsewhere it is repeated in full at the end of each stanza.

## (a) INTRODUCTION

1. *MS. Advocates Library 18.7.21.* (1372) ; printed in Carleton Brown's *Religious Lyrics of the Fourteenth Century* (Oxford, 1924), p. 71.

2. *MS. Bodley 29734, Eng. Poet. e. 1.* (1460-1480) ; printed in Thomas Wright's *Songs and Carols . . . from a Manuscript of the Fifteenth Century* (Percy Society, 1847), p. 20.
l. 2. *Hangèd*, MS. *hang*.

3. *MS. British Museum Sloane 2593* (*c.* 1450) ; printed in Wright's *Songs and Carols from a Manuscript in the British Museum of the Fifteenth Century* (Warton Club, 1856), p. 94.

4. *Eng. Poet. e. 1.* ; Wright, *Percy Society*, p. 50. Also in *Sloane 2593* ; Wright, *Warton Club*, p. 48.

5. Printed in G. England and A. W. Pollard's *The Towneley Plays* (*Early English Text Society, Extra Series LXXI,* 1897), p. 139. Mr. Pollard suggests 1410 as the date of the *Second Shepherds' Play* and 1460 as the date of the MS.

6. Robert Bridges' *The Testament of Beauty* (Oxford, 1929), III, ll. 403-405.

## (b) TEXT

I. The poems of *MS. British Museum Harley 913*, written in the Anglo-Irish dialect, have been associated with the name of Friar Michael Kildare, *e.g.* by Carleton Brown in his *A Register of Middle English Religious and Didactic Verse* (Oxford, 1920), i, 308. J. E. Wells, however, suggests that they were ' composed probably in or about the Abbey of Kildare in

Ireland, by emigrants from Southern or South-Western England ' (*A Manual of the Writings in Middle English* (Yale U.P., 1916), p. 228). I have preferred to mark the poem ' anonymous.' Wells dates the MS. *c.* 1308-1318, or at the latest before 1325 ; Brown places it shortly after 1329.

II and III are taken from a commonplace book compiled in 1372 by an unidentified Franciscan, John Grimestone. Whether he composed or merely copied these lullabies cannot be determined.

III. The first three stanzas appear in a slightly differing form in *MS. British Museum Harley 7322* (latter half of fourteenth century) and are reprinted in F. J. Furnivall's *Political, Religious, and Love Poems* (*E.E.T.S., Original Series 15*, 1866), p. 255.

Carleton Brown prints I, II, III in his *Religious Lyrics of the Fourteenth Century*, pp. 35, 83, 91.

IV. Wright *Percy Society*, p. 12.

11. *MS. byrd* emended to *bryd*, to rhyme with *betyde* ( = *betid*).

I have adopted the following readings from Richard Hill's *Balliol MS. 354* (1508-1536), edited by R. Dyboski in *Songs, Carols, and other Miscellaneous Poems* (*E.E.T.S., Extra Series CI*, 1908 for 1907), p. 25 :

1, 2. *nyght—sight* ; Bodley *nyghth—syghth.*

8. *thus gan she say* ; Bodley *sayd.*

10. *hay* ; Bodley *hayd.*

19. *I am knowen as hevyn kyng* ; Bodley *I bekydde am kyng.*

21. *thowgh* ; Bodley *thar.*

64. *And if* ; Bodley *If.*

V. *The Pageant of the Shearmen and Taylors* was printed by Thomas Sharp, in *A Dissertation on the Pageants or Dramatic Mysteries Anciently Performed at Coventry* (Coventry, 1825), from a sixteenth century MS. since destroyed by the burning of the Free Reference Library at Birmingham in 1879. The MS. was written, and the ' matter neuly correcte,' by Robert Croo, who completed his task on March 14, 1534. Sharp's reprint was edited by Prof. J. M. Manly in his *Specimens of the Pre-Shakespearian Drama* (Boston, 1897), and his text is now generally adopted.

VI. Little is known of John Phillip, or Phillips, except that he was a member of Queen's College, Cambridge, and the author of a number of tracts, elegies, and ballads as well as of the play from which this lullaby is taken. His works were published between 1566 and 1591.

**XI.** This is ascribed to Stephano Felis by Nicholas Yonge in his *Musica Transalpina* (1588), a collection of Italian madrigals ' translated most of them five years ago [*i.e.* in 1583], by a Gentleman for his private delight ' (Dedicatory Epistle to Gilbert, Lord Talbot). It is not clear whether Stephano Felis was the composer of the words, or of the tune, or of both words and tune of the Italian original.

**XIII.** The text is modernised from that given in the *Percy Folio MS.*, with the addition of ll. 3-4 from Elizabeth Rogers' *Virginal Book*, 1658 (*MS. British Museum Addit. 10,337*). The full refrain runs :

> ' Balow, la-low, la-la-la, ra-row, fa-la, la-la,
> La-la, la-la-la, la-low ! '

In his *Reliques of Ancient English Poetry* (London, 1876), ii, 211-213, Thomas Percy Scotticises all the English words and substitutes for the Folio MS. title *Balowe* the misleading heading *Lady Anne Bothwell's Lament. A Scottish Song.* The poem, however, is purely of English origin, and there is no justification for the identification of the singer with Lady Anne Bothwell, which was first made by Watson in his *Comic and Serious Scots Poems* (Edinburgh, 1711).

Mr. Chappell, in a valuable note contributed to J. W. Hales and F. J. Furnivall's edition of the Folio MS. (London, 1868, iii, 522), assigns *Balow* to the sixteenth, not, as previous critics had done, to the seventeenth century. Other early versions of this popular poem occur in Richard Brome's *The Northern Lass,* for which see XXVII, and in the MSS. of Pinkerton (*c.* 1625-1649), John Gamble (1649) and Elizabeth Rogers (1658). It was also printed in an amplified form as a street ballad under the title of *The New Balow* [London, 1670 ?].

**XVI.** *Patient Grissell* was entered in Henslowe's Diary as early as 1599. It is generally agreed that Dekker contributed the lyrics, including this favourite lullaby written for Janicola to sing while Babulo rocks the cradle.

**XVII.** The full poem, as it originally appeared in R[obert] V[erstegan]'s *Odes. In Imitation of the Seaven Penitential Psalmes* (Antwerp, 1601), runs to twenty-four stanzas, of which only the first four—the best—are here reprinted. For the *my lives joy* of the refrain of the 1601 edition I have substituted *mine only joy*, as given in the abbreviated version in Martin Peerson's *Private Musicke* (1620).

**XIX.** A shorter version is printed by A. H. Bullen, in *More Lyrics from the Song-Books of the Elizabethan Age* (London,

1888), p. 73, from *MS. British Museum Addit. 17790.* This version was set to music by William Byrd (1540-1623).

XXIII. A slightly longer version occurs in *MS. Christ Church 87,* and will be found in Mr. Norman Ault's *Seventeenth Century Lyrics* (Longmans, 1928), p. 16.

The dates of performance or composition assigned to Jacobean and Caroline plays are those suggested by F. G. Fleay in his *A Biographical Chronicle of the English Drama, 1559-1642* (London, 1891).

XXIX. In *The Jealous Lovers* these two stanzas are sung by Tyndarus and Techmessa respectively over the swooning Sexton and his wife, before the latter are placed in the coffins from which the singers have just risen. If their dramatic setting be forgotten, they provide an interesting example of the lullaby of the ' terrifying ' order.

XXXI. I have adopted Mr. Ault's date (*c.* 1640) for the British Museum MS., although the binding merely describes it as seventeenth century. Mr. Ault was, I believe, the first to print XXV, XXXI, and XXXV (*op. cit.*). In each case I have consulted the manuscript original.

XXXIV. Five regular eight-line stanzas, in which the Cavalier idealistically anticipates peace while not forgetting to make financial recompense to the lady, complete the poem.

XL. Compare XV.

XLI. Joseph Warton borrows the first four lines from the *Ode to Sleep* of his father, Thomas Warton the Elder (1688-1745), whose *Poems on Several Occasions* he edited in 1747. The *Ode to Sleep* begins :

> O gentle, feather-footed Sleep,
> In drowsy dews my temples steep,
> Softly waving o'er my head
> Thy care-beguiling rod of lead.

I have tentatively dated Joseph's *Ode c.* 1747 in view of the probability that the borrowing was made when the son was at work on the father's poems. The fact that Joseph issued no collection of his own lyrics after his *Odes on Various Subjects* (1746) would help explain the posthumous first appearance of this little piece in Chalmers.

XLIV. The following note on *The Highland Balou* is given in W. E. Henley and T. F. Henderson's *The Poetry of Robert Burns* (Edinburgh, 1901), iii, 429 :

123

'The MS. is in the Hastie Collection. Stenhouse states that it is " a versification, by Burns, of a Gaelic nursery song, the literal import of which, as well as the air, were communicated to him by a Highland lady." But there are humorous touches in it which the original (if there was an original) could not have shown.'

XLVII. The Latin inscription was first published, as from ' A Correspondent in Germany,' in *The Morning Post*, Boxing Day, 1801. The English translation first appeared with the Latin original in *The Courier*, August 30, 1811, with the following introductory note :

' About thirteen years ago or more, travelling through the middle parts of Germany I saw a little print of the Virgin and Child in the small public house of a Catholic Village, with the following beautiful Latin lines under it, which I transcribed. They may be easily adapted to the air of the famous Sicilian Hymn, *Adeste fideles, laeti triumphantes*, by the omission of a few notes ' (E. H. Coleridge : *The Complete Poetical Works of Samuel Taylor Coleridge* (Oxford, 1912), i, 417-418, notes, 2, 3).

LI. In a note to this poem Scott says : ' These words, adapted to a melody somewhat different from the original, are sung in my friend Mr. Terry's drama of Guy Mannering.' Daniel Terry's dramatisation was first acted at Covent Garden on March 12, 1816, and the lullaby, as sung in Act II, Scene i, by Miss Bertram, is a short two-stanza song. So far as I have been able to ascertain, the poem as it stands in the text first appeared in *The Poetical Works of Walter Scott, Esq.* (Edinburgh, 1820), x, 174. In modern collected editions it is dated 1815, perhaps because the novel *Guy Mannering* was first published in that year ; but the *Lullaby* does not appear in the novel.

LVI. The title is from *Poems. By Elizabeth Barrett Barrett* (London, 1844). In *Graham's Magazine* the poem had appeared under the title *The Child and the Watcher*.

LVIII. *Sweet and Low* is one of the six songs that were first added in the third edition of *The Princess* (1850). In l. 6 the 1850 version reads ' *dropping* moon.'

Tennyson originally made two versions of this song and sent them to his wife to choose which should be published. The unpublished version, which in her opinion was less song-like, is given in Hallam Lord Tennyson's *Alfred Lord Tennyson. A Memoir* (London, 1899), p. 212.

# INDEX OF AUTHORS

Anonymous, I-V, X, XI, XIII, XVIII, XIX, XXII, XXV, XXXI, XXXV.

Ayres, Philip, XXXVIII.

Barnes, William, LXII.
Blake, William, XLII, XLIII.
Breton, Nicholas, XIV (?).
Brome, Richard, XXVII.
Browning, Elizabeth Barrett, LIII, LVI.
Burns, Robert, XLIV.

Campion, Thomas, XXI.
Cartwright, William, XXX.
Clough, Arthur Hugh, LX.
Coleridge, Samuel Taylor, XLVII.
Coleridge, Sara, LII.
Cotton, Charles, XXXVI, XXXVII.

Dekker, Thomas, XVI.
Denham, Sir John, XXXIII.

Fletcher, John, XX.

Gall, Richard, XLV.
Gascoigne, George, VII.
Goffe, Thomas, XXIII, XXIV.
Greene, Robert, XII.

Hogg, James, XLVIII, LIV.

Jordan, Thomas, XXXIV.

Keats, John, L.

Longfellow, Henry Wadsworth, LVII.

Mabbe, James, XXVI.

Phillip, John, VI.

Quarles, Francis, XXVIII.

Randolph, Thomas, XXIX.
Rogers, Samuel, XLIX.
Rossetti, Christina Georgina, LXI.
Rowlands, Richard, XVII.

Scott, Sir Walter, LI.
Shakespeare, William, XV.
Sidney, Sir Philip, VIII, IX.
Swinburne, Algernon Charles LXIII (i-vii).
Symonds, John Addington, LXIV.

Tennyson, Alfred, Lord, LV, LVIII, LIX.

Verstegan, Robert, see Rowlands, Richard.

Warton, Joseph, XLI.
Warton, Thomas, the Younger, XL.
Watts, Isaac, XXXIX.
White, Henry Kirke, XLVI.
Wither, George, XXXII.

Yeats, William Butler, LXV.

125

# INDEX OF FIRST LINES

Asleep !  O sleep a little while, white pearl !  -  L.

Baby, baby bright  -  -  -  -  -  -  LXIII (i).
Baby, baby dear  -  -  -  -  -  -  LXIII (ii).
Baby, baby fair -  -  -  -  -  -  LXIII (v).
Baby, baby kind  -  -  -  -  -  -  LXIII (vi).
Baby, baby sweet  -  -  -  -  -  -  LXIII (iii).
Baby, baby true  -  -  -  -  -  -  LXIII (iv).
Baby, baby wise  -  -  -  -  -  -  LXIII (vii).
Baloo, baloo, my wee wee thing  -  -  -  XLV.
Balow, my babe, lie still and sleep !  -  -  -  XIII.
Bawloo, my bonnie baby, bawlillilu  -  -  -  LIV.
Be still, my blessed Babe, though cause thou hast
    to mourn  -  -  -  -  -  -  -  X.
Be still, my sweet sweeting, no longer do cry  -  VI.
Bring a light, the foe's in sight  -  -  -  -  XXXIV.

Calmly as the morning's soft tears shed  -  -  XXXI.
Care-charming Sleep, thou easer of all woes  -  XX.
Close now thine eyes, and rest secure  -  -  XXVIII.
Come, little babe, come, silly soul  -  -  -  XIV.

Dormi, Jesu !  Mater ridet  -  -  -  -  XLVII.
Drop golden showers, gentle sleep  -  -  -  XXIII.

Golden slumbers kiss your eyes -  -  -  -  XVI.

Hee balou, my sweet wee Donald  -  -  -  XLIV.
Hush, my bonny babe ! hush, and be still !  -  XLVIII.
Hush ! my dear, lie still and slumber  -  -  XXXIX.

Ler to loven as I love the -  -  -  -  -  III.
Lips, lips, open !  -  -  -  -  -  -  LX.
Lock up, fair lids, the treasure of my heart  -  VIII.
Lo here, beneath this hallow'd shade  -  -  XL.
Lollai, lollai, litil child, Whi wepistou so sore ? -  I.
*Lullaby baby, lullaby baby*  -  -  -  -  VI.
Lullaby, lullaby baby, Great Argos' joy  -  -  XXIV.
Lullaby, oh, lullaby !  -  -  -  -  -  LXI.

*Lulla la, lullaby!* - - - - - - X.
Lullay, lullay, litel child! Child, reste the a
   throwe - - - - - - - II.
*Lully, lulla, thow littell tinë child* - - - - V.

My little sweet darling, my comfort and joy - XIX.

Now sleep, and take thy rest - - - - XXVI.

O gentle, feather-footed Sleep - - - - XLI.
O hush thee, my babie, thy sire was a knight - LI.
O sisters too, How may we do - - - - V.
O sleep, my babe, hear not the rippling wave - LII.

Peace, wayward bairn! O cease thy moan! - XXVII.

Quiet, sleep! or I will make - - - - XXIX.

Seal up her eyes, O sleep, but flow - - - XXX.
See how like twilight slumber falls - - - XXXVI.
She sleeps. Peace crown thine eyes! Sweet
   dreams in deep - - - - - XXXV.
Sing lullaby, as women do - - - - VII.
Sleep, angry beauty, sleep, and fear not me - XXI.
'Sleep, baby mine, Desire!' Nurse Beauty
   singeth - - - - - - IX.
Sleep, baby mine, enkerchieft on my bosom - XLVI.
Sleep, baby, sleep! The Mother sings - - LXIV.
Sleep, Ellen Aubrey, sleep, and dream of me - LV.
Sleep, happy boy, there sleep and take thy rest XXXVIII.
Sleep on, and dream of Heav'n awhile - - XLIX.
Sleep on, baby, on the floor - - - - LVI.
Sleep! sleep! beauty bright - - - - XLIII.
Sleep, sleep, mine Holy One! - - - - LIII.
Sleep! Sleep! mine only jewel - - - XI.
Sleep, sleep, my soul, let sorrow close thine eyes XXV.
Sleep, sweet babe! my cares beguiling - - XLVII.
Somnus, the humble god that dwells - - XXXIII.
Sweet and low, sweet and low - - - - LVIII.
Sweet babe! true portrait of thy father's face - LVII.
Sweet baby, sleep! What ails my dear? - XXXII.
Sweet dreams, form a shade - - - - XLII.
Sweet was the song the Virgin sung - - - XXII.

The angels are stooping - - - - - LXV.
The rook's nest do rock on the tree-top - - LXII.

This lovely lady sat and song - - - - IV.
*Thys endris nyght I saw a sight* - - - - IV.

Upon my lap my sovereign sits - - - - XVII.

Weep not, my wanton, smile upon my knee - XII.
Weep you no more, sad fountains - - - XVIII.
What does little birdie say - - - - LIX.
Winds, whisper gently whilst she sleeps - - XXXVII.

You spotted snakes, with double tongue - - XV.

PRINTED IN GREAT BRITAIN BY ROBERT MACLEHOSE AND CO. LTD.
THE UNIVERSITY PRESS, GLASGOW